Russ's background is in medicine. He qualified as a doctor in 1989, at the University of Newcastle-Upon-Tyne in the UK. He emigrated to Australia in 1991, and set up practice as a GP in Melbourne.

As a GP he became increasingly interested in the psychological aspects of health and wellbeing (and increasingly disenchanted with writing prescriptions). Ultimately this interest led to a total career change, and he now works in two different, yet complementary roles: as a therapist and as a life coach.

Over the years, he has trained in many types of therapy and coaching, but when he discovered Acceptance & Commitment Therapy, (ACT), a unique and creative mindfulness-based behavioural therapy, he was so deeply impressed that he immediately went to the USA to train with its creators, Steve Hayes, Kelly Wilson, and Kirk Strosahl. Since then, he has been back many times, and is now an internationally renowned ACT trainer. His ACT-based self-help book is a bestseller, now published in over twenty-two countries and seventeen different languages.

Since 2005, Russ has travelled all around Australia, and internationally, providing workshops and training for a wide variety of health professionals, from coaches and counsellors, to psychologists and psychiatrists. His highly-acclaimed ACT workshops are typically brief, powerful, cost-effective and life-enhancing. Participants regularly report not only major improvements in their therapy and/or coaching, but also in their personal lives – and evaluation forms frequently praise his ability to make complex ideas seem very simple.

D1579342

Touching the _elephant_
within with closed eyes
Draw by touch
Da Vinci's mind.

elephant within = Da Vinci
mind = Art Therapy =
eyes closed - touch =
develop visualization
skills = manifestation
skills -

THE
REALITY
SLAP

& Filling the Gap

DR RUSS HARRIS

is the hero's journey
Mindfulness & VALUES
& Cultivation

ROBINSON

Constable & Robinson Ltd
55–56 Russell Square
London WC1B 4HP
www.constablerobinson.com

Published in Australia in 2011 by Exisle Publishing Limited.

First published in the UK by Robinson,
an imprint of Constable & Robinson Ltd, 2012

A copy of the British Library Cataloguing in
Publication data is available from the British Library

ISBN: 978-1-78033-202-4

Printed and bound in the UK

1 3 5 7 9 10 8 6 4 2

Important Note
This book is not intended as a substitute for medical advice or
treatment. Any person with a condition requiring medical attention
should consult a qualified medical practitioner or suitable therapist.

DEDICATION

To my beautiful son. At the time of writing you are only five years old, and yet, you are by far my greatest teacher. Thank you for teaching me so much about living and loving; for helping me to grow and develop; for bringing so much joy and love into my life. I love you more than words can ever hope to express.

Contents

Introduction

THE SLAP AND THE GAP

When was the last time you received a reality slap? We've all had plenty of them in our lives: those moments when life suddenly deals us a painful blow. It's a shock, and it hurts, and it knocks us off balance; we struggle to stay on our feet, and sometimes we fall.

The reality slap takes many different forms. Sometimes it's so violent, it's more like a punch: the death of a loved one, a serious illness or injury, a freak accident, a violent crime, a disabled child, bankruptcy, betrayal, fire, flood or disaster. At other times the slap is somewhat gentler: that sudden flash of envy when we realise someone else has got what we want; those sharp pangs of loneliness when we realise how disconnected we are from others; that burst of anger or resentment over some sort of mistreatment; those short, sharp shocks when we catch sight of our reflection and we don't like what we see; those painful stabs of failure, disappointment or rejection.

Sometimes the slap quickly recedes into memory: a passing moment, a brief 'rude awakening'. At other times it knocks us senseless and leaves us wandering in a daze for days or weeks. However, whatever form it takes, one thing's for sure: the reality slap hurts. We don't expect it, we don't like it, and we definitely don't want it. And, unfortunately, the slap is just the beginning. What comes next is much harder. For once the slap wakes us up, we then face *the gap*.

I call it 'the reality gap' because on one side is the reality we have, and on the other is the reality we want. And the bigger the gap between those two realities, the more painful the feelings that will arise: envy, jealousy, fear, disappointment, shock, grief, sadness, anger, anxiety, outrage, dread, guilt, resentment; perhaps even hatred, despair or disgust. And, whereas the slap is usually over quickly, the gap can persist for days, weeks, months, years and even decades.

Most of us are ill-equipped to deal with large reality gaps. Our society doesn't teach us how to handle them or, rather, it doesn't teach us how to handle them effectively, in such a way that we can thrive and find lasting fulfilment. Our first instinct, whenever we encounter a reality gap, is to try and close it; we take action to change reality, so it conforms to our wishes. And if we succeed, the gap closes and we feel good. We feel happy, content or calm, with a sense of achievement or relief. And this is all well and good. After all, if there's something we *can* do to get what we want in life — and if it's not a criminal activity, and it doesn't go against our core values, and it's not going to create even bigger problems for us — then it makes sense to go ahead and do it.

But what happens when we *can't* get what we want? What do we do when we *can't* close that reality gap; when someone we love dies, or our partner leaves us, or our kids move overseas, or we can't have children, or our child has a serious disability, or someone we want to be friends with doesn't like us, or we lose our eyesight, or we are diagnosed with an incurable or chronic illness, or we're not as smart or talented or good-looking as we would like? And what happens when we *can* close the reality gap, but it's going to take a long, long time to do it; how do we cope in the meantime?

I once read an article that claimed all self-help books could be lumped into two categories: those that claim you can have everything you ever wanted in life, if only you put your mind to it; and those that claim you *can't* have everything you want, but you can still lead a rich and rewarding life. This book is definitely in the second category.

To be honest, I am amazed that people buy books in the first category. If you look closely at anybody's life, from Bill Gates to Brad Pitt, from Buddha to Jesus, from the rich and famous and powerful to the beautiful and strong and smart, you will see that nobody gets everything they want. It is impossible. During our time on this planet, we're all going to experience disappointment, frustration, failure, loss, rejection, illness, injury, ageing and death.

If the reality gap is small, or it seems like we can close it relatively quickly, then most of us handle it reasonably well. But the bigger it gets, and the longer it stays open, the more we tend to struggle. And this is why 'inner fulfilment' is so important. Inner fulfilment is a deep sense of peacefulness, wellbeing and vitality that you can experience even in the face of a large reality gap: even when your dreams don't come true, your goals aren't achieved and your life is harsh, cruel or unfair.

This is very different to 'external fulfilment': those good feelings we have when we manage to conform reality to our wishes; to close the gap, to achieve our goals, to get what we really want in life. External fulfilment is important: we all like to achieve goals and get our needs met. But external fulfilment isn't always possible. (If you think it *is* always possible, you're definitely reading the wrong book. You should read one of those books that claim you can have whatever you want simply by asking the Universe and believing it will deliver.)

In this book, then, as you've probably gathered, we're going to focus on inner fulfilment: a deep sense of wellbeing and peace that we cultivate from within ourselves, rather than searching for it outside ourselves. And the good news is, the resources that enable inner fulfilment are always available to us; they're like a bottomless well deep inside us, from which we can draw whenever thirsty. However, just because this is our focus, it doesn't mean we give up on all our worldly pleasures, desires, wants, needs and goals; we'll certainly look at how to close the reality gap, if and when it can be closed. What it *does* mean is that we no longer depend upon things outside ourselves for our sense of wellbeing and vitality; that even in the midst of great pain, or fear, or loss, or deprivation, we can find a sense of peace and comfort within.

Twenty-two Blind Men

You probably know the old story about the three blind men and the elephant. Just to refresh your memory, three blind men approach the ringmaster of a circus. 'We want to know what an elephant is like,' they say. 'Can you let us touch one?' The ringmaster agrees and allows them to touch his prize elephant who, luckily, is very friendly and accommodating. The first blind man grabs the elephant's trunk and feels it all over. 'Gosh,' he says, 'an elephant is just like a python.' Meanwhile, the second blind man is running his hands all over the elephant's leg. 'It's nothing like a python,' he protests, 'it's like a tree trunk.' At the same time, the third blind man is feeling the elephant's tail and says, 'I don't know what you two are talking about. An elephant is like a piece of rope.'

Of course, all three men were accurate in their observations, but each one of them held only one piece of the puzzle. And this book is somewhat similar: I liken it to *twenty-two* blind men exploring an elephant. Each chapter will bring you into contact with one aspect of the elephant — sometimes a large part, like the trunk, and sometimes a smaller detail, like an eyelid. Eventually, by the end of the book, the elephant will be revealed in all its glory. (I even thought about calling this book *The Elephant Within* but it just didn't have the same ring.)

The elephant in question is called Acceptance and Commitment Therapy or ACT (which is said as the word 'act', not as the initials). ACT is a scientifically based model for enriching and enhancing human lives, created by US psychologist Steven C. Hayes, based on the concepts of mindfulness and values. If you're new to these concepts and how they help us thrive in the face of life's challenges, then this book will give you a gentle but thorough introduction. But, if you are already familiar with these concepts, then this book will help you to gain new insights, remind yourself of the things you had forgotten, or revisit old places and discover something you hadn't previously noticed.

The chapters in this book are designed not only to open up your mind, but also your heart. In some I'll be playful and light-hearted, and in others I'll be deadly serious and share deeply personal stories that may even bring a tear to your eyes. I like to think of each chapter as windows opening on to a magnificent landscape: they enable you to appreciate where you are; they extend your view, allowing you to see further and more clearly; and they open up possibilities for new directions.

So please take your time and enjoy the journey. There is no need to rush. Each time you touch the elephant, savour that contact; each time you open a window, appreciate the view. In this way, step-by-step, and moment-by-moment, you will learn how to find fulfilment when reality hurts.

PART I

AFTER THE SLAP

Filling the Gap – with
the elephant within.
Focus on elephants.

Chapter 1

THE FOUR STEPS

I didn't see it coming. Around the time of my fortieth birthday, reality was treating me so well, I thought, 'Maybe life *really does* begin at forty!' Everything seemed to be going my way. After twenty years of writing and five unpublished novels, my first book was finally about to be published. I loved my work as a therapist and life coach, and my career was heading off in new and exciting directions. I had excellent health, a strong marriage and wonderful friends. But all of that paled in comparison to the greatest joy in my life: my beautiful baby boy, who was then eleven months old. I have never known anything like those overwhelming feelings of love, joy and tenderness that a parent feels towards a child.

Like most new parents, I thought my son was the most beautiful, intelligent baby in the whole wide world — and I often fantasised about his future life. He would be so much smarter than me in every way — and unlike me, he would excel at sport, be super popular with all his schoolmates, and be a big hit with the girls when he got older. Then he would naturally go on to university and develop some high-power career. Ahh, the wonders of 'fantasy land'.

By the time our son was eighteen months old, my wife and I were concerned that he was lagging behind in his developmental milestones. Among other things, he wasn't walking, and he had very few words. So we took him to a paediatrician and had him assessed. The paediatrician checked him out thoroughly and assured us he was just 'slow' to develop, as 'boys often are'. He told us not to worry and to come back and see him if we had any more concerns.

Well, three months later, our concerns had grown significantly. Our son still had very few words, still wasn't walking, and seemed to understand very little of what we said to him. So we took him back to the specialist. More tests followed: two hours of intensive assessment. And again the specialist told us there was nothing wrong: our little boy was just slow to develop; he would soon catch up; nothing to worry about.

Over the next two months, we became increasingly worried. Our son often seemed 'spaced out' in his own private world. He was almost two years old now and still not walking. He was getting around by shuffling on his bum; it looked cute and funny, but it troubled us. And he had started some odd behaviours, such as rolling his eyeballs, grinding his teeth and staring out of the corner of his eyes at parallel lines on walls and floors. He was still hardly speaking and he did not even seem to know his own name.

So we went for a second opinion. The new paediatrician was very concerned and immediately arranged for a thorough assessment, which included a speech therapist and a psychologist. And just five days before my beautiful baby boy turned two, he was diagnosed with autism.

My world crumbled. I have never felt such pain in all of my life.

'Autism' is one of those words like 'cancer' or 'AIDS': when you hear it in everyday conversation, you can't help but shudder. And when you hear it as a diagnosis applied to your own child, it's like someone sticking a knife into your gut and twisting it around, and then slowly pulling your intestines out through the wound. *gutted* –

I cried, I sobbed, I howled. I didn't know it was possible to hurt so much. I've broken bones, been seriously ill, and witnessed loved ones die, but the pain of those events was miniscule compared to this.

* * *

Dr Elisabeth Kübler-Ross famously described the 'five stages of grief' as denial, anger, bargaining, depression and acceptance. Although she was specifically referring to death and dying, these stages also apply to all types of loss, shock, crisis and trauma. However, they are not discrete and well-defined stages, and many people don't experience all of them. Also, there is no fixed order in which these stages occur. They frequently happen simultaneously; they tend to ebb and flow and blend into one another; and often they seem to 'end' and then 'start again'.

For reality slaps of a less violent or dramatic nature, you might not experience any grief, but for major crises and losses, you almost certainly will go through at least some of these stages, so let's briefly discuss them.

'Denial' refers to a conscious or unconscious refusal or inability to acknowledge the reality of the situation. This could manifest as unwillingness to talk about it or think about it; or as trying hard to pretend that it's not happening; or as a pervasive sense of unreality — walking around in a daze, feeling as if it's all just a bad dream.

In the 'anger' stage, you might get angry with yourself, or others, or life itself. And, of course, anger has many close relatives that frequently drop in: resentment, indignation, fury, outrage, or a strong sense of unfairness, injustice or betrayal. *Rage* –

'Bargaining' means attempting to strike deals that will alter the reality; this might include anything from asking God for a reprieve, to asking a surgeon to guarantee the operation will be successful. It frequently involves lots of wishful thinking and fantasising about alternative realities: 'If only *this* had happened', 'If only that *hadn't* happened'.

Unfortunately, the 'depression' stage is misnamed. It does not mean experiencing the common clinical disorder known as 'depression'. Rather it refers to the normal emotions of sadness, sorrow, regret, fear, anxiety and uncertainty, which are natural human reactions to loss and trauma.

Finally, the 'acceptance' stage refers to making peace with the reality gap, instead of struggling with it or avoiding it.

In the months that followed my son's diagnosis, I found I went through all of these 'stages' many times over. At the time of writing this book, it has been more than three years since that reality slap, and I have learned and grown much during that time. And although the slap is now a distant memory, the reality gap it unveiled still remains open. Therefore, as we go through this book, I will share with you my journey, to illustrate many of the principles within these pages. I have to say, at risk of it being a cliché, that although my journey has been long and hard and painful, it's also been incredibly rewarding. Along the way, there's been a huge amount of sadness, fear and anger, but there's also been plenty of joy, love and wonder, and I fully expect that you will find the same on your own journey.

Of course, your reality gap may seem very different to mine — and also to those of other people you know. Divorce, death or disability; illness, injury or infirmity; depression, anxiety or addiction: they all *seem* to be very different from one another but, beneath the surface, they are all very similar. In each case, we face a big gap between the reality that we've got and the reality that we want. And the bigger that gap is, the bigger the pain. And the bigger the pain, the less effectively we cope. So in this book, I'm going to outline a strategy that will help you deal with any sort of reality gap, no matter how great or small, and no matter whether it's temporary or permanent. This strategy will help you to close that gap, if and when it can be closed, and to find inner fulfilment when it can't be closed (either temporarily or permanently).

Basically, this strategy involves four steps:

- Hold yourself kindly. & *lightly*
- Drop the anchor.
- Take a stand.
- Find the treasure.

Let's take a quick look at these now.

Step 1: Hold Yourself Kindly

Compassionate Brain Heart

When we're hurting, we need to be kind to ourselves. Unfortunately, this is easier said than done. For most of us, the default setting of our mind is to be harsh, judgemental, uncaring or self-critical (this is especially likely if you believe that you created your own reality gap).

We all know self-criticism doesn't help us, but that doesn't stop it from happening. And popular self-help approaches, such as challenging our negative thoughts, or repeating positive affirmations, or practising self-hypnosis, do not work for most of us in the long term; our minds continue to be harsh, judgemental and self-critical. So we need to learn the art of self-compassion: how to hold ourselves kindly and gently. We need to learn how to support and comfort ourselves, and how to

TAI-CHI ✗ re-parent
MINDFULNESS

handle our painful thoughts and feelings effectively, so they have less impact and influence over our lives.

Yoga – Tai-chi – Breath work – ARTWORK

Step 2: Drop the Anchor *GROUNDING*

The larger the reality gap, the greater the emotional storm it unleashes within. Waves of painful feelings crash through our bodies and painful thoughts blow wildly through our heads. When we get carried away by this storm of thoughts and feelings, we are helpless; there is nothing we can do but desperately try to save ourselves from drowning. So when that storm hits us, we must drop anchor and ground ourselves, so we can take effective action. Dropping anchor doesn't get rid of the storm; it just holds us steady until the storm passes.

ATTITUDE

Step 3: Take a Stand *STANCE WARRIOR TAI-CHI.*

Whenever we encounter a reality gap, it helps to ask ourselves this question: 'What do I want to stand for in the face of this?' We can stand for giving up on life, or we can stand for something far more meaningful. We can stand for something that matters, deep in our heart: something that dignifies our suffering and gives us the will and the courage to carry on.

Obviously, we can't turn back time. We can't undo whatever it is that has happened. But we can choose the attitude we take towards it. Sometimes when we take a stand, we can close the gap, and at other times, obviously we can't. But the moment we take a stand, we experience vitality; we may not have the reality we want, but we do have the satisfaction of living with purpose.

Step 4: Find the Treasure

Once we have put the first three steps into practice, we will be

Literature.

in a very different space mentally. And from this space, we will be able to find and appreciate the many treasures life has to offer. This last step may sound impossible, especially if you are currently in the midst of great anxiety, sadness or despair — but it is not. To give you a dramatic example, a few years ago a friend of mine suffered a tragic loss: her three-year-old daughter died suddenly from septicaemia. It was the most heartbreaking funeral I'd ever attended: an outpouring of grief without end.

What amazed and inspired me over the ensuing months was the way my friend continued to find fulfilment. In the midst of her unimaginable sorrow, tormented and shattered by her loss, she did not lose touch with all that remained in her life. At the same time as making room for her grief, she reached out and connected with her family and friends, her work, her religion and her creativity. And, in doing so, she found love, joy and comfort. Her pain did not disappear; I doubt it ever will. Her reality gap did not close; how on earth could it? But she was able to appreciate the reality _around_ that gap; to appreciate how much life still had to offer.

If you don't have children yourself, you may not realise just how remarkable this is. Personally, I can't think of anything worse than losing a child. Many parents become severely depressed or suicidal under these circumstances. But it doesn't have to be that way. We do have a choice, even though our minds often say that we don't.

This then, is the final step of our journey: to find the treasure buried beneath all our pain. That doesn't mean we deny the pain is there, or we try to pretend that it doesn't hurt. Rather, it means we acknowledge the pain is there _and_ we also appreciate all that life has to offer.

At this point, you may notice your mind protesting. It may insist that your case is different to everyone else's; that your life will remain pointless, empty, miserable or unbearable unless your reality gap is closed. If so, rest assured: those are perfectly natural thoughts that many people have when they're new to this approach. And if I try to convince your mind that its comments are wrong, I will almost certainly lose. For example, I could start quoting the vast amount of research on ACT (Acceptance and Commitment Therapy), much of it published in leading psychological journals, which shows it is effective with everything from depression and addiction, to reducing stress at work and dealing with a terminal diagnosis of cancer. But your mind could easily dismiss all this with one comment: 'That doesn't mean it will work for me.' And I can't argue with that. There's a very good chance this approach will help you, but I can't *guarantee* it. However, I *can* guarantee that if you stop reading simply because your mind says, 'This won't work', then you definitely *won't* get any benefit from this book!

So, how about we just let your mind have its say? Let it tell you whatever it wants, but don't let it stop you. Let it chatter away like a radio playing in the background while you keep on reading, and see if you can be curious about where this leads you. Because although our minds like to think they can predict the future, really . . . who knows what might happen?

Chapter 2

PRESENCE, PURPOSE AND PRIVILEGE

As Burrhus Frederic Skinner, one of the most influential psychologists in human history, lay on his deathbed, his mouth grew dry. When a carer gave him some water, he sipped it gratefully, then uttered his final word: 'Marvellous'.

Inspiring, isn't it? To think that even on his deathbed, with his organs failing, his lungs collapsing and leukaemia running rampant through his body, B.F. Skinner could enjoy one of life's simple pleasures.

This true story contains three important themes relevant to every human being who seeks inner fulfilment. No matter how you travel this path, whether through modern Western scientific approaches such as ACT, or through ancient Eastern spiritual approaches such as Buddhism, Taoism or yoga, you will encounter three core themes I call the three P's: Presence, Purpose and Privilege.

Presence

If we wish to find lasting fulfilment, we must develop the ability to live fully in the present moment. However, to stay fully present — engaged in and open to our here-and-now experience — is not easy. Why? Thanks to that wonderful gift we are all born with: the human mind. Minds are wonderful things — we'd be in trouble without them — but if you've got one, then you can't help but notice that it never stops thinking. The mind churns out thoughts all day long, and often we get 'hooked' by them and pulled out of our life. Most of us walk around lost in our thoughts for large parts of the day, missing out on our experience in this moment. And many of us fail to even realise it.

For example, have you ever done something like this? You get into the shower, the warm water hits your body and, for a moment or two, you're fully present: fully engaged in the rich sensual experience of the shower. The water flows down your back, the warmth soothes your muscles, your body hums with pleasure. And then . . . within the space of a few seconds, you drift off into your thoughts: 'What's on the to-do list for today?' 'Oh, I have to get that project completed.' 'Oh no, I forgot to tell Susan about the girl's night.' 'What will I make Timmy for lunch today?' 'Only three more days until we go on holiday, yippee!' 'Hmmm. Getting a bit chubby around the waist, better start exercising again.'

As you get more and more drawn into your thoughts, the shower progressively recedes into the background. You know the shower is still happening, but you're no longer fully engaged in it. It's more like your body is over there, taking the shower on autopilot, while you're over here having a fabulous conversation inside your head. And then, before you know it, the shower is over.

Most of us, if we're honest, spend large chunks of our day lost in our thoughts, wandering around in a veil of 'psychological smog' and, consequently, we miss out on much of the richness of life. This is all the more likely when we face a large reality gap; our minds churn out no end of painful thoughts and we easily get 'pulled in'. For example, if reality dumps something dramatic and unexpected on our doorstep — a sudden death, a divorce or a disaster — we may wander around in a daze, unable to 'think straight', or remember properly, or even perform our routine tasks adequately.

Furthermore, the ability to engage fully in what we are doing, and keep our attention on the task, is essential for mastering any skill or activity, and vital for effective action of any kind. So if we wish to respond effectively to whatever painful blow life has dealt us, we have to be 'present'.

(Note: 'Presence' is more commonly known as 'mindfulness' and, throughout this book, I will use the two terms interchangeably. Mindfulness is currently a hot topic in Western psychology, and in textbooks and self-help books you'll almost always find its origins attributed to Buddhism. However, this is a major misconception. Buddhism is only 2,600 years old; mindfulness is much older than that. We can find it in Judaism, Taoism and yoga, going back around 4,000 years. Indeed, the Buddhist scriptures make it clear that the Buddha originally learned the art of mindfulness from a yogi! In this book, we will approach mindfulness, or presence, from a Western scientific tradition — ACT — which has plenty of similarities to these ancient approaches, but also many differences.)

Purpose

'Yes, yes,' people will sometimes say, 'it's all very well, being present, but what do I do with my life?' This is a very important question. Much as a flower needs sunlight, presence needs purpose; otherwise we run the risk of being fully present in a life that lacks meaning.

One of the greatest challenges we all have to face is discovering what we want our lives to be about. What sort of human beings do we want to be? What do we want to stand for in our brief time on this planet? Towards what ends do we wish to invest our time and energy?

Of course, some people are happy to go along with the purpose imposed upon them by their religion, family or culture — but for most of us, this is not the case. Most of us have to create that sense of purpose for ourselves — a task easier said than done. The more we can connect with a purpose that guides our actions now and in the future, the more we will experience a sense of fulfilment; we will feel we are making the most of our time on this earth.

For some of us, when a huge reality gap opens, it actually helps us to clarify our purpose in life: we get in touch with 'the big picture', we reflect on what life is all about, we connect with our core values, and we grow and develop. We may even discover a cause or create a mission, which ignites our passion and gives us a sense of vitality. For others, though, it has the opposite effect: our minds may react strongly against the gap and claim that life is pointless, hopeless or unbearable. And if we get hooked by these thoughts, all purpose is lost: life becomes a burden, it has no point. So if we want to take a stand in the face of this gap, we need to be in touch with what really matters; we need to know what our values are, so we can create and draw on a sense of purpose.

Privilege

When wood and fire combine within the hearth, they provide us with a wonderful experience of warmth. And when purpose and presence combine within our heart, they provide us with a wonderful experience of privilege. A privilege means a special benefit, or an advantage granted only to the few. When we experience life as a privilege, something to be appreciated and relished, rather than taking it for granted or treating it as a problem to be solved, then naturally it is far more fulfilling. We all pay lip service to the notions that life is 'short', 'precious' or 'a gift', but all too often, lost in our thoughts, adrift from our purpose, we fail to truly appreciate what we have in this moment.

This is especially likely during times of great suffering. Our minds may well protest, 'It's not fair!' 'Why me?' 'I can't stand this', 'Why is life so hard?' 'It shouldn't be like this!' 'I can't carry on any longer', or even, in severe cases, 'I want to die'. And yet, believe it or not, even in the midst of great adversity, it is possible to treat life as a privilege and make the most of it. (And as I said in the previous chapter, if your mind protests that this is not possible for you, just let it chatter away like a radio playing in the background, and carry on reading.)

Skinner's Deathbed

The story of Skinner's final word neatly illustrates the three P's. Even on the verge of death — and reality gaps don't get much bigger than that — he was fully present, able to savour that last sip of cold water. As for purpose, Skinner's whole life was devoted to helping humans lead better lives. (This was something he achieved in abundance: his theories and research revolutionised Western psychology and strongly influenced many contemporary models of therapy, coaching and personal development.)

Was this same sense of purpose present to him on his deathbed? Well, we can only speculate. But it seems to me that the very same purpose (helping others) extended to the utterance of his final word. After all, what was the point of saying 'marvellous', if not to inspire and comfort his loved ones during a time of great suffering?

And as for the third of the three P's, did he not beautifully model what it means to treat this life as a privilege and make the most of the opportunities it affords us?

This story is relevant to all of us. How often do we fail to appreciate what we have? How often do we take life for granted? How often do we miss out on the marvels and miracles of human existence? How often do we amble through life on autopilot, without any clear sense of purpose guiding our actions? How often do we get so caught up in our problems, fears, losses and regrets that we forget about all the good stuff in our lives?

Now don't worry — I'm not going to go all airy-fairy on you and pretend that life is all sweetness and roses and we can all live happily ever after. The undisputable fact is that life is difficult and it involves plenty of pain. And no matter how good it gets, sooner or later, if we live long enough, we'll face a huge reality gap. However, as well as the pain and hardship, there is also much to savour, appreciate and celebrate — even if we're in the midst of great grief or enormous fear. Yet we will not be able to do this without first applying the principles of presence and purpose. (And that is why 'positive thinking' — telling yourself that every cloud has a silver lining — is highly unlikely to help you if it's your main strategy for dealing with pain; in fact, as we'll see later, there's a good chance it will make your pain worse in the long term!)

Obviously if someone is in truly dreadful circumstances — living in a concentration camp, or being tortured in a prison, or starving in the Ethiopian wilderness — there will be very little to savour or appreciate; but if you are reading this book, clearly that is not your situation. Still, to some readers, it may seem that your situation is just as bad or almost as bad as those mentioned, and the last thing I want to do is debate that with you. All I ask you to do is to keep an open mind; you don't have to *believe* that any or all of these three P's are possible. Just read the book and be curious about what happens.

For now, my aim is solely to heighten your awareness. So what I invite you to do is this: as you go about your day, notice when and where the three P's occur. For example, after the death of a loved one, many of us experience all three P's at the funeral. At times, we are very engaged in the ceremony (presence); at times, our words and actions are loaded with purpose; and at times we are grateful for the kindness and love of others (privilege). So whatever you are grappling with in your life, notice when these moments happen.

When and where are you fully present and engaged in what you are doing? When and where are you aligned with purpose and doing what truly matters to you? When and where do you experience a sense of privilege: embracing and appreciating life as it is in this moment?

Also notice how you help to create these moments and how they contribute to your life. This simple act of noticing can make a vast difference. It might not seem like much, but as we shall see, it forms the very foundation of inner fulfilment.

NOTICE

PART 2

HOLD YOURSELF KINDLY & LIGHTLY.

↓

1 Anatomy of Breething
2 photo reced —
3 Read without glasses
4 Tai chi--

Beware of the Wolves (dressed up) disguised as sheep like New Age spirituality. a massive Industry that makes billions on selling "luciferian light" 2 "poor fuckers" like me & you -

see ; Law of Attraction. quantum collapse ....etc that deny the FIRST foundational noble Truth that life is suffering & avoiding it is Reinforcing it

Acceptance = compassion.

Chapter 3

A CARING HAND

When reality slaps you hard and leaves you reeling, what do you want from the people you love? Most of us want pretty much the same thing. We want to know there is someone there for us: someone who truly cares about us; someone who takes the time to understand us; someone who recognises our pain and appreciates how badly we are suffering; someone who will make the time to be with us and allow us to share our true feelings, without expecting us to cheer up or put on a brave face and pretend everything is okay; someone who will support us, treat us kindly and offer to help; someone who demonstrates through their actions that we are not alone.

What we generally find, when we face a big reality gap, is that some people respond to our pain very well, in ways such as those listed above but, alas, there are many who do not. Think about the last time something incredibly painful, hurtful or stressful happened in your life. What kind of responses did you get that made you feel truly cared for, supported, accepted and understood? Below are a few responses that would meet these criteria for most people. (Keep in mind, we are all individuals, and different situations require different responses; not everyone wants to be treated in the same way, and there is no one response that is appropriate for all situations under all circumstances.)

- Giving you a hug, embrace or a cuddle.
- Holding your hand.
- Placing an arm around you.
- Validating your pain: 'This must be so hard for you' or 'I can't begin to imagine what you're going through' or 'I can see you're in terrible pain'.
- Saying nothing, just sitting with you and allowing you to be.
- In some circumstances, such as a painful loss, they may hold you while you cry, or even cry with you.
- Offering support: 'Is there anything I can do to help?'
- Asking how you feel.
- Sharing their own reactions: 'I'm so sorry' or 'I'm so angry' or 'I feel so helpless. I wish there was something I could do' or even 'I don't know what to say'.
- Creating space for your pain: 'Do you want to talk about it?' or 'It's okay to cry' or 'We don't have to talk. I'm happy just to sit here with you'.
- Giving support unconditionally, such as making dinner for you, or taking care of your kids, or helping you out with your daily tasks.
- Making the effort to actually come and visit you, and spend some time with you in person.
- Genuinely listening, as you tell them about what you're going through.
- Saying something like, 'I'm here for you' and genuinely meaning it.

These sorts of responses all send the same message: I'm here for you, I care about you, I accept you, I understand you, I see you're in pain, and I want to help. There are many, many ways of delivering this message, some more eloquent than others. For example, when my son was first diagnosed, my pain was almost unbearable and one of the most wonderful responses came from my best friend, Johnny. Now Johnny's a very down-to-earth sort of guy, so when he caught up with me, a few days after the diagnosis, he gave me a big strong hug and said, 'You poor f***er! You must be feeling so f***ing shit!' These are hardly poetic words, but they were said with such warmth and kindness, they touched me far deeper than the most eloquent of poems ever could.

However, truly compassionate responses can be quite rare. This is largely because people often just don't know how to respond — society hasn't taught us what to do. Quite commonly, you will encounter people doing some of the following (and if we're honest, almost all of us have said and done things like this at times — I know I have!):

- Quoting proverbs at you: 'Plenty more fish in the sea', 'Time heals all wounds', 'Every cloud has a silver lining'.
- Telling you to 'think positively'.
- Asking about your situation, but then quickly changing the subject.
- Giving advice: 'What you should do is this', 'Have you thought about doing such and such?'
- Trumping your pain: 'Oh yes, I've been through this many a time myself. Here's what worked for me.' *BRUCE*
- Telling you to get over it: 'Build a bridge', 'Move on', 'Let it go', 'Isn't it time you got over this?'
- Discounting your feelings: 'No use crying over spilt milk', 'It's not that bad', 'Cheer up!', 'Stiff upper lip'.
- Telling you your thoughts are irrational, or that you do too much negative thinking.
- Trivialising or diminishing your pain: 'Put into perspective, there are kids starving in Africa . . .'
- Trying to distract you from your pain: 'Let's get drunk!'

'Let's go out and have some fun', 'Let's eat some chocolate', 'Let's watch a movie'.

- Not coming to visit or spend time with you, or even actively avoiding you.
- Playing 'Mr Fix-it': coming up with all sorts of helpful solutions for your problem.
- Saying they want to help, but not following up.
- Listening impatiently.
- 'Putting up' with or tolerating your distress, but not truly accepting it.
- Reassuring you: 'It'll be all right, you'll see', 'It's not as bad as you think', 'You'll get through this'. (Note: Many people see reassurance as a compassionate act — and it can be at times — but the problem is, it easily puts the 'reassurer' in a 'one up' position, like a parent reassuring a young child.)
- Giving you factual information related to the issue, and/or strategies to deal with it, without first asking about how you feel.
- Trying to minimise your pain: 'You'll look back on this and laugh', 'A year from now, this will be a distant memory'.
- Insulting you: 'You're making a big deal out of nothing', 'Take it like a man', 'Grow up!'
- Blaming you: 'You brought this on yourself', 'If you hadn't done X, Y and Z, then this would never have happened', 'I warned you this would happen'.
- Ignoring you.

While some responses on the second list are rude or offensive, most of them are genuine attempts to help. However, most of us, when we are on the receiving end of such responses, are likely to feel hurt, irritated, rejected, invalidated, unappreciated, misunderstood or offended. For example, when my son was diagnosed, someone said to me, 'God gives special children to special parents.' I was furious. Although this person was coming from a good place, genuinely trying to say something helpful, they spoke way too soon; they had not first made an attempt to acknowledge or recognise or empathise with my pain. Because of this, I had no sense that they understood what I was going through, and I did not feel supported or cared for. It sounded to me like a glib comment, devoid of understanding and compassion — and deep down, underneath my fury, I was actually very hurt and very sad.

Clearly some of those responses in list two, such as constructive problem solving and practical advice, can actually be very helpful — but only if they come *at the right time* and if they are *preceded* by caring and empathy. For example, all my books are dotted with well-known quotes and, *at the right time*, these quotes are generally uplifting and inspiring. However, if they are the first thing you say to someone who has just been slapped by reality, you will come across as uncaring or offensive. Suppose that a person you love greatly has just died and the very first thing someone says to you is, 'Well, what does not kill you makes you stronger!' or 'Those things that hurt also instruct!' How would you feel?

As a general rule, a compassionate response, such as those on the first list, must come before anything else. If someone leaps in with advice, proverbs, positive thinking or action plans, without first demonstrating their compassion, we are likely to feel upset, annoyed, offended, hurt or irritated — often without quite realising why.

When we are hurting, most of us want to feel understood, accepted and cared for *before* we are ready to start looking for solutions or strategies, or new ways of thinking about a situation. *After* we feel understood, accepted and cared for, we may *then* be grateful for some of those responses on list two. But obviously not for the offensive ones — when someone blames us, or minimises our problems, or tells us that we should be stronger, naturally we will feel even worse.

Now here are some questions for you to reflect on:

- Who is the one human being in your life who can always be there for you, in any moment, no matter what happens?
- Who is the one human being who can understand, validate and empathise with your pain, better than anyone else on the planet?
- Who is the one human being who can truly know just how much you are suffering?

You are.

So, you are in a unique position. No matter how tough things get in your life, *you* are always there; even if no one else is available, *you* are; and *you* can always do something to help (even if your mind says you can't).

Building a good relationship with ourselves is essential for inner fulfilment, especially when we run into a large reality gap. Unfortunately, this does not come naturally. Most of us are not too good at accepting, appreciating, nurturing, supporting, encouraging and being compassionate towards ourselves. Far more commonly, we beat ourselves up, judge ourselves harshly or neglect and give up on ourselves. And sadly, when we encounter those big reality gaps, we tend to rush straight to strategies from the second list above, rather than choosing compassionate responses from the first one. Check this out for yourself: read through both lists again and estimate how often you respond to yourself from list two, as opposed to list one.

***

Now suppose for a moment, you could change this relationship with yourself; that you could become your own best friend. (Your mind may say this sounds corny or impossible, but if you take a leap of faith and keep reading, you'll eventually see that it's neither. For now, just let your mind have its say.) Once you learn how to do this, you're in a wonderful position. Why? Because wherever you go, whatever you do, no matter how big the reality gap you encounter, your 'best friend' will be there to support you: to be compassionate when you're suffering, understanding when you get it wrong, and encouraging when you lose heart.

Finding Self-compassion

At the end of *Casablanca,* Humphrey Bogart mutters the classic line, 'Louis, I think this is the beginning of a beautiful relationship.' And when we first start to learn about self-compassion, it is the beginning of a beautiful relationship with ourselves. The word 'compassion' is derived from two ancient Latin words: *com* meaning 'together' and *pati* meaning 'suffering'. Thus 'compassion' literally means 'suffering together'. However, these days the meaning is more complex: it means noticing the suffering of others, with a spirit of kindness and caring, and a genuine desire to help, give or support.

Compassion for ourselves is essential for inner fulfilment; when reality slaps us around, we need all the kindness we can get. But for most of us, this is easier said than done. When we fail, or get rejected, or make mistakes; when we catch ourselves acting in ways we do not approve of; when we believe that we have contributed to our reality gap: then the mind's natural tendency is to beat us up. It likes to pull out a big stick and give us a hiding; to kick us when we're already down. It may tell us we're not being strong enough, or we should be handling things better, or that others are far worse off than we are, so we really have nothing to complain about. It may tell us to get a grip, or sort ourselves out. It may even tell us that we're pathetic, or we only have ourselves to blame for what has happened.

For example, when someone we love dies, the mind may blame us for not having loved them enough, or not having been there enough, or not having told them enough how much we loved them; and sometimes even for not having prevented their death! One of my clients even blamed himself for surviving a plane crash. His mind told him it was not fair that he had lived when twelve other passengers had died: a classic case of 'survivor guilt'. (And when my son was diagnosed with autism, my mind blamed me for passing on faulty genes.)

Even if the mind doesn't launch into a personal attack, it is often callous, cold and uncaring; and rather than help us cope, it crushes our spirit. It may tell us we can't cope, or that life's not worth living; or it may remind us, over and over, of just how unfairly life has treated us; or it may conjure up terrible fears about what's to come. So if we can learn how to hold ourselves kindly, we'll be much better off. We'll have a sense of support, comfort and encouragement, which will make us much better equipped to handle the gap.

I'd like to give you a taste of self-compassion right now. I find that some men initially resist the following exercise because they think it is 'girly' or 'weak' or 'touchy feely'. But once they get past those judgements and give it a go, they invariably find it helpful.

A Compassionate Hand

I invite you now to find a comfortable position, in which you are centred and alert. For example, if you're seated in a chair, you could lean slightly forwards, straighten your back, drop your shoulders and press your feet gently on to the floor.

Now bring to mind a reality gap you are struggling with. Take a few moments to reflect on the nature of this gap: to remember what has happened, to consider how it is affecting you, and to think about how it might impact your future. And notice what difficult thoughts and feelings arise.

Now pick one of your hands and imagine it's the hand of someone very kind and caring.

Place this hand, slowly and gently, on whichever part of your body hurts the most. Perhaps you feel the pain more in your chest, or perhaps in your head, neck or stomach? Wherever it is most intense, lay your hand there. (If you're numb, lay your hand on the part that feels the numbest. If you're feeling neither pain nor numbness, then simply rest your hand on the centre of your chest.)

Allow your hand to rest on you, lightly and gently; feel it against your skin or against your clothes. And feel the warmth flowing from your palm into your body. Now imagine your body softening around this pain: loosening up, softening up and making space. If you're numb, then soften and loosen around that numbness. (And if you're neither hurting nor numb, then imagine in any way you like, that in some magical sense your heart is opening.)

And hold your pain or numbness very gently. Hold it
as if it is a crying baby, or a whimpering puppy, or a
priceless work of art.

Infuse this gentle action with caring and warmth —
as if you are reaching out to someone you care about.

Let the kindness flow from your fingers into your
body.

Now use both of your hands in one kind gesture.
Place one hand on your chest and the other on your
stomach. Let them gently rest there, and hold yourself
kindly. Take as long as you wish to sit in this manner,
connecting with yourself, caring for yourself,
contributing comfort and support.

Continue this for as little or as long as you wish: five
seconds or five minutes, it doesn't matter. It's the
spirit of kindness that counts when you make this
gesture, not the duration of it.

* * *

Most people find this exercise very soothing. It tends to centre
them and bring comfort. So I encourage you to do it repeatedly
throughout your day. (Obviously this wouldn't go down well
in the middle of a business meeting; it is best to keep this as
something you do in private!) And if by some chance you didn't
get much out of it, please try it again, at least several more times.
With repetition, you are likely to find it very helpful.

Also feel free to adapt or modify this exercise. For example,
if you don't like placing your hands as suggested above, you can

substitute any gesture of kindness you prefer: rubbing your neck or shoulders, massaging your temples or your eyelids, gently stroking your forehead or arm.

This simple act of self-compassion can have a profound impact if you practise it often. Think of it as 'emotional first aid': the very first step you take when you are hurting.

2

The Two Elements

Self-compassion consists of two main elements and so far we've only looked at the first one: being kind to ourselves. In later chapters, we'll explore self-kindness in more depth, but for now we're going to focus on the second element: being present with our pain.

Now notice your mind's reaction to the previous sentence. Is it saying something like: 'But I don't want to be present with my pain! I want to get away from it!'? If your mind has reacted this way, that's to be expected; it reflects a common misunderstanding of presence. You see, presence (which you'll recall is also known as 'mindfulness'), involves a new way of responding to our pain; it dramatically lessens the impact of painful emotions and it liberates us from the smog of painful thoughts. And if you don't have a clue what that means, I hope you'll be patient, because over the next few chapters you'll find out.

Chapter 4

BACK TO THE PRESENT

Ali, an Iraqi refugee, had been horribly tortured under Saddam Hussein's regime. Because he had dared to publicly criticise the government, he had been thrown into prison for several months, and during that time, his jailers had done the most horrific things to his body. Two years later, as he sat on the other side of my office, Ali kept having 'flashbacks' to those events. A flashback is a memory that is so vivid and incredibly real, it's as if it is actually happening here and now. If you've never had one, you can scarcely imagine how terrifying it can be.

Whenever Ali tried to talk to me about his time in prison, a flashback would hijack him; his body would go rigid, his eyes would glaze over, and his face would go pale and sweaty. Dragged back into the past, he would relive the torture as if it were happening again. So my first task, before addressing any of his other serious problems, was to teach him how to get himself back to the present.

Now although Ali's case is dramatic, it is similar in nature to the challenge we all face whenever a large reality gap opens. The mind has many different ways to hijack our attention. As with Ali, it may pull us back into the past, replaying the painful events that opened the gap, or it may push us into the future, conjuring up all manner of fearful scenarios. It may even drag us deep into the swamp of our current problems: bogging us down in our pain and our stress and our hardship. For example, in the first week after my son was diagnosed, I was consumed by a thick black smog of rage, despair and fear; totally lost in thoughts such as 'It's not fair' and 'Why me?' and 'If only'. I was furious with reality: how could it treat me this way? I ranted and raved about the unfairness of life: *How could this happen? How come some parents, who are totally unfit for the role of parenthood, get healthy normal children that they don't even want?*

But while it's perfectly normal for our minds to react this way, it is not particularly helpful. We can't respond effectively to a reality gap while we're lost inside a smog of painful thoughts. So the first thing we need to do is learn how to bring ourselves back into the present. And we do this by using a skill I call 'connection'.

Connection

'Connection' is one of the three core skills involved in presence. (The other two are called 'defusion' and 'expansion', and we'll get to them in the next few chapters.) Connection means engaging fully in your experience: paying full attention, with openness and curiosity, to what is happening in the here and now.

Think of life as an ever-changing stage show. On that stage are all your thoughts and feelings, and everything that you can see, hear, touch, taste and smell. Connection is like bringing up the lights on the stage in order to take in the details: at times, shining a spotlight on a particular performer, at other times illuminating the entire stage.

Connection is essential for effective action. If we want to do anything well, from dancing and skiing, to making love and conversation, to stacking dishes and playing cards, we need to keep our attention on the task at hand. The more we get entangled in our thoughts, the less attention we pay to what we are doing, and the more ineffectively we act. Our performance suffers; we make mistakes; we do things badly. We've all experienced this many times, in hundreds (if not thousands) of different activities.

And here's the thing: no matter what sort of reality gap we face — a terminal illness, infidelity, obesity, bereavement, social isolation or unemployment — some sort of action is required. So, if we want to act effectively, we need to pull ourselves out of our thoughts and connect with the world around us. The following exercise shows you how to do this. I call it 'Be Like A Tree', and I like to do it at least two or three times a day. However, when I'm very stressed, I do it far more often.

Be Like A Tree

Think of a mighty tree: its long roots stretching deep into the ground below, its sturdy trunk rising upwards, and its branches stretching into the sky above. Use this image to inspire you as you follow the steps below.

STEP 1. ROOTS

Whether you are standing or sitting, plant your feet firmly on to the floor. Get a sense of the ground beneath you and gently press your feet downward. Notice the pressure of the ground against your soles and the gentle tension in your legs. Straighten your spine and let your shoulders slide down your back. Get a sense of gravity 'flowing' down your spine, into your legs and feet, and into the ground below. It's as if you are taking root in the earth and 'planting' yourself firmly.

STEP 2. TRUNK

Slowly draw your attention upwards from the roots to the trunk (it is no coincidence that your abdomen and chest are called the 'trunk' of your body). Maintain some awareness of your feet against the floor, but focus mainly on your trunk. Sit up in your chair, or stand up straight, and notice the change in your posture. Breathe slowly and deeply, and notice the rise and fall of your rib cage. Note the gentle heaving of your shoulders and the rhythm and movement of your abdomen. Empty your lungs completely, then allow them to refill by themselves. Now expand your awareness: notice your whole trunk at the same time — your lungs, chest, shoulders and abdomen. Do this for at least ten breaths; if you have more time, do fifteen or twenty.

STEP 3. BRANCHES

Just as the branches of a tree reach into the sky, you now reach out into the world around you. Activate all five senses and extend them in all directions: notice, with curiosity, what you can see, hear, smell, taste and touch. Maintain some awareness of your roots and trunk, and the background rhythm of your breathing, but focus your attention *mainly* on the environment. Get a sense of where you are and what you are doing. Smell and taste the air as you breathe it in. Notice five things you can feel against your skin, such as the air on your face, the shirt on your back or

> the watch on your wrist. Notice five things that you
> can see and pay attention to their size, shape, colour,
> luminosity and texture. Notice five things that you
> can hear: the various sounds of nature or civilisation.
> Now engage fully in whatever task you are doing,
> giving it all your attention.

***

The 'Be Like A Tree' exercise takes anything from three to six minutes to complete, depending on how many breaths you take in Step 2. And, as a general rule of thumb, the greater your emotional pain, the longer you should do it. And, if you like, you can add in the 'Compassionate Hand' exercise as described in the previous chapter. If you wish to do this, then in Step 2 of the exercise above, you would place a hand gently on your body and 'send yourself' kindness and warmth. This helps to infuse the exercise with self-compassion.

Now you probably found that despite your best intentions your mind repeatedly pulled you out of that exercise; it hijacked you and bundled you off before you even realised it. (If that *didn't* happen, you're either lucky or you're already good at this skill.) In the following chapters, we'll look at how and why the mind does this and what we can do about it.

In the meantime, practise this exercise every day, ideally two or three times. And even if at first it seems to make little difference, persist. Over time, it will pay great dividends. And if your mind gets impatient for results, then remember these words, which come from the great Scottish author, Robert Louis Stevenson:

> *Don't judge each day by the harvest you reap,*
> *but by the seeds that you plant.*

Chapter 5

HIS MASTER'S VOICE

Can you hear it? That voice inside your head? The one that virtually never shuts up? There's a popular misconception that folks who 'hear voices' are abnormal in some way, but we all have at least one voice inside our head, and most of us have quite a few! For example, most of us have at times been embroiled in an inner mental debate between the 'voice of reason and logic' and the 'voice of doom and gloom', or the 'voice of revenge' and the 'voice of forgiveness'. And we're all familiar with that self-judgemental voice that is often called the 'inner critic'. (I once asked a client, 'Have you heard of the "inner critic"?' 'Yes', she said, 'I've got an inner committee!')

Obviously the ability to think is incredibly valuable, and it adds enormously to our quality of life. Without the ability to think, we could neither create nor appreciate books, movies, music or art; nor could we enjoy blissful daydreams, or plan for the future, or share our feelings with loved ones. However, a lot of our thoughts are not particularly useful. Suppose I plug into your mind, record all your thoughts for the next twenty-four hours and transcribe them on to paper. Then I ask you to read through the transcript and highlight any thoughts that had been *truly helpful* for you to respond effectively to the reality gap.

What percentage of the thoughts on that paper do you think you would highlight?

For most of us, the percentage would be pretty small. It's almost as if the mind has a mind of its own; it seems to talk all day long about whatever it pleases, with little regard as to whether this helps us or not. In particular, it seems to be very fond of dwelling on pain from the past or worrying about the future or obsessing about the reality gap in the present. And yet, even though what it has to say is often unhelpful, somehow it almost always manages to absorb us in its stories.

Now before we go any further, let me clarify what I mean by 'stories' because from time to time, when I use this word with my clients, somebody gets offended. 'They're not *stories*,' this person is likely to protest, 'they're *facts*!' To which I reply, 'I'm sorry if you are in any way offended, but what I mean by "story" is a sequence of words or pictures that conveys information. I could use the more common term "thoughts", or the technical term "cognitions", but calling them "stories" helps us to handle them more effectively. You see, our mind tells us all sorts of stories all day long. If they are "true stories" we call them "facts", but facts make up only a tiny percentage of our thoughts. Our thoughts include all sorts of ideas, opinions, judgements, theories, goals, assumptions, day-dreams, fantasies, predictions and beliefs that can hardly be called "facts". So, the word "story" doesn't imply that the thoughts are false or inaccurate or invalid — it's simply a way of describing what thoughts are: words or pictures that convey information.'

I will be using the term 'story' frequently throughout this book, but if you don't like it, replace it in your head with the technical term 'cognition' or the everyday term 'thought'.

Now consider this: how often does your mind keep you awake at night or consume huge chunks of your day with stories that induce guilt, fear, anger, anxiety, sadness, disappointment or despair? How often does it pull you into stories of blame, resentment, worry or regret? How often does it get you stressed out, wound up, angry or anxious, in a manner that makes your situation even harder?

If your answer to the last three questions is 'very often', then that shows you have a normal human mind. Yes, I did say 'normal'. That's what normal human minds naturally do. Eastern philosophers have known this for thousands of years but, somehow, in the West, we have bought into the idea that when the mind operates this way it is abnormal. This is very unfortunate because it sets us up to struggle with our minds (which is futile) or to judge ourselves harshly for the way we think (which is also futile). So I encourage you to take a different perspective. Let's think of our minds as master storytellers that don't care if their stories are helpful or not; their main aim is to capture our attention.

Have you ever seen the famous painting that formed the logo for *His Master's Voice* — a once-renowned record label? The image shows a small white dog (his name was Nipper) listening with great fascination to an old wind-up gramophone as he hears a recording of his deceased master's voice. Nipper is so intrigued by that voice he is virtually sticking his head down the funnel of the gramophone. We are a bit like that dog; our mind speaks and we give it all our attention. The difference between us and that dog is that the dog will soon lose interest in the voice; he will realise it has nothing to offer him and he will go off and do something more interesting. But when it comes to our minds, we generally *don't* lose interest. Even if we've heard this recording ten thousand times, and all it does is make us miserable, we *still* readily become fixated by it.

A Smoky Haze

We have many ways of talking about this human tendency to get 'absorbed' or 'caught up' in our thoughts. We may use colourful metaphors such as 'He's a million miles away', or 'Her head's in the clouds' or 'He's lost in thought', or we may talk of worrying, ruminating, rehashing the past, stressing out, going over and over it, or being preoccupied.

Basically, this incredibly valuable, uniquely human ability to generate thoughts can leave us wandering around in a smoky haze, absorbed in our thoughts and missing out on life.

Of course, to be in a smoky haze is not necessarily bad. The smoky haze of incense sticks can be soothing and relaxing. The smoky haze of a bonfire can be exhilarating and fun. But what happens when the smoke gets too thick? You start to cough, your nose runs and your eyes water. And over time, if you keep on breathing in all that smoke, you will eventually damage your lungs.

Similarly, there's a time and place where being absorbed in our thoughts is life-enhancing: daydreaming on a beach, mentally rehearsing an important speech, creating new ideas for a project. But most of us get the balance wrong; we spend way too much time inside our minds, and we wander through our days in a thick cloud of 'psychological smog'.

And there's nothing that thickens the smog like a large reality gap. The greater the discrepancy between what we've got and what we want, the more our minds protest. They generate a ceaseless torrent of unhelpful thoughts and may go into denial: 'This can't be happening'; get angry: 'This shouldn't have happened!'; go into despair: 'I can't cope. I'll never get over this'; agonise over the unfairness of it all; compare our life to others and find it wanting; or conjure up all the possible worst-case scenarios. And as I've said before, these patterns of thinking are all very normal, but they're not of much help to us.

But before we go any further, let's make one thing clear: *our thoughts are not the problem*. Our thoughts do not create the psychological smog. It is *the way we respond* to our thoughts that creates the smog.

Our thoughts are simply pictures and words in our heads. Don't take my word for this; check it out for yourself. Stop reading, and for one minute, close your eyes and notice your thoughts. Notice where they seem to be located, whether they are moving or still, and whether they are more like pictures, words or sounds. (Sometimes your mind goes shy when you attempt this; your thoughts disappear and refuse to come out. If this happens, just notice the empty space and the silence inside your head and wait patiently. Sooner or later your mind will start up again, even if only to say, 'I haven't got any thoughts!')

* * *

What did you notice? If your mind went blank at first, then you would have noticed an empty space and silence, but eventually some thoughts showed up, and presumably they were words or pictures or both. (If you noticed a sensation or a feeling in your body, then that's exactly what it is: a 'sensation' or 'feeling'. Don't confuse these things with 'thoughts'.)

When we allow these words and pictures to come and go freely, to flit through our awareness like birds in the sky, they create no problems. But when we clutch them tightly and refuse to let them go — *that* is when they turn into smog; *that* is when they pull us out of our life.

When we're lost in that smoky haze, all the details are obscured and all the richness is lost. We can't taste the sweetness for the smoke. There could be the love of our life on the other side of that smog, there could be the greatest show on earth, but we wouldn't know it.

If you've ever spent time with someone who was severely

depressed (perhaps yourself, at some point in your life), you know how impenetrable that cloud can be. In our society, the depressed person is typically surrounded by all sorts of opportunities to enhance and enrich their life, but they are completely unable to see it, choking in the smog of despair. (This is not *always* true, of course, but often it is.)

I'll give you a personal example. One evening, about two weeks after my son was first diagnosed, I drove down to the beach to clear my head. While driving to the beach, I started to imagine my little boy's future. My mind conjured up all sorts of dreadful scenarios: mental retardation, rejection, teasing, bullying, victimisation, isolation, becoming one of society's forgotten people. By the time I set foot on the sand, I was living a nightmare. And as I walked along the beach, it grew worse and worse. Well, after about half an hour of this nightmare, I suddenly gasped. I stopped in my tracks and fell silent, gazing in awe at one of the most magnificent sunsets I have ever seen. The sun had disappeared behind the horizon and the sky had erupted like a volcano: furious clouds of crimson, scarlet, gold and orange. I just stood there and watched for several minutes, without saying a word, unable to believe I had missed this transformation.

There are many different types of smoky haze. When we're in the thick of one, not only are we missing out, we're also fumbling; the thicker the haze, the more difficult it becomes to navigate our course, negotiate the obstacles and rise to our challenges. In ACT we have a technical name for this state — 'fusion'. Just as sheets of molten metal fuse together, so we become fused with our thoughts. And in this state of fusion our thoughts have an enormous impact on us: they may seem to be the absolute truth, or commands we must obey, or threats we must eliminate, or something we have to give all our attention to.

However, when we *defuse* from our thoughts, they lose all

their power over us. *Defusion* means we separate from our thoughts and see them for what they are: nothing more or less than words and pictures. In a state of defusion, our thoughts may or may not be true, but whether they are or not, we don't have to obey them, we don't have to give them all our attention, and we don't have to treat them as a threat. In a state of defusion we simply 'step back' from our thoughts and 'disentangle' ourselves from them. We see them for what they are — words and pictures — and we let them be. We loosen our grip on them and allow them to come, stay and go in their own good time.

And, of course, if our thoughts are *helpful* — if they help us to be kind and compassionate to ourselves, or to clarify our values and make effective plans and take effective action to enrich and enhance our lives in practical ways — then we make good use of them. We won't let them *control* us, but we'll certainly let them *guide* us. When we adopt this approach, we are rarely concerned as to whether or not our thoughts are true: what we're far more interested in is if they are helpful. If we hold on tightly to these thoughts, if we get all caught up in them, if we let them push us around and dictate what we do, then will that *help* us to adapt to the situation, to make the most of it and to behave like the person we want to be? If our thoughts are helpful we *use* them, and if they're unhelpful we *defuse* them.

The Art of Noticing

The very first step in defusion is something you have already been practising: noticing. The instant we notice we're in a smoky haze, it immediately starts to clear. You see, when we are totally fused with our thoughts, we are not even aware that we're thinking. The difference between *real* smog and psychological smog is that when we're stumbling around in the *real* stuff, we know about it: it's hard to breathe, hard to see and hard to walk. But when we're lost in psychological smog, we often fail to realise it. For example, sometimes we can be caught up in worrying, resentment, or analysing our problems for hours on end. (Have you ever gone for a drive and been so caught up in your thoughts that you remembered virtually nothing about the journey? Or reached the end of a page, but can't recall reading it?)

Thus the first step in defusion is simply *to notice* that we are fused (i.e. lost in, absorbed by, or preoccupied with our thoughts). This is a bit like suddenly glimpsing your reflection in a mirror and being surprised at your appearance; or catching and righting yourself just as you trip; or abruptly realising, in the middle of a conversation, that you haven't been listening to the other person and now you have no idea what they are talking about. It's an 'Aha!' moment; a gentle jolt, like suddenly waking up from a snooze.

The moment we notice we are fused, we need to defuse — to get present and snap out of the trance. There is more to defusion than this (and we'll discuss this later in the book), but this act of noticing your own fusion is always the first step. So I invite you to practise it throughout the day to see how often you can catch yourself in the act. See if you can discover when and where are you most likely to get lost in the smog: in your car, riding your bike, at work, lying in bed, after dinner, playing with your kids, having a shower, or when talking to your partner. And what kinds of smog do you tend to get lost in: worrying, resentment, daydreaming, blaming, self-criticism, wishful thinking, dwelling on problems, reliving horrors from the past, predicting the worst, thinking your life is over?

Also notice what sort of events precipitate a smog: an argument, a driver cutting you off, a rejection, a failure, an unfair or dismissive act, a tight deadline, a great opportunity, a particular expression on somebody's face, a provocative comment, a piece of good news, a piece of bad news, a song, a movie, a photograph, the mention of a loved one?

And finally, once you get out of your smoky haze, notice where you are and what you're doing, and acknowledge what you've been missing out on.

Most of us are surprised when we first start to realise just how much time we spend lost in the smog. And, unfortunately, our minds often give us a hard time about it: 'I don't believe it. I did it again. What's wrong with me? Why do I keep doing this? Why can't I just snap out of it?' And if we're not careful, we then get fused with a whole bunch of thoughts about how we shouldn't be fused! Can we find some humour in this? Can we silently chuckle to ourselves, as we recognise our similarity to that little dog listening to his master's voice?

Chapter 6

PAUSE THE MOVIE

William Shakespeare is often quoted thus: *There is nothing either good or bad, but thinking makes it so.* This is a common belief in many forms of popular psychology: that our thoughts can somehow make things good or bad. That is why so many approaches encourage you to get into a battle with that voice in your head. They tell you to challenge, dispute or invalidate those 'negative' thoughts and replace them with 'positive' ones — and it's certainly a seductive proposition! It appeals to our common sense: stomp on the 'bad' thoughts and replace them with 'good' ones. But the problem is, if we start a war with our own thoughts, we will never win. Why? Because there's an infinite number of those so-called 'negative' thoughts, and no human being has ever managed to find a way of eliminating them.

Zen masters, who are like the Olympic athletes of mind training, know this all too well. There's a classic Zen tale about an eager monk who asks his abbot, 'How can I find the greatest Zen master in the land?' The abbot replies, 'Find the man who claims he has eliminated all negative thoughts. And when you find this man . . . you know that's not him!'

Yes, we can all learn to think more positively, but that won't stop our minds from generating all sorts of painful, unhelpful stories. Why not? Because learning to think more positively is like learning to speak a new language; if you learn to speak Swahili, you won't suddenly forget how to speak English.

So if our only way of dealing with those 'negative' stories is to battle with them — to challenge them in terms of whether they are true or false; to try and disprove them; to try to push them away, suppress them or distract ourselves from them; or to try to drown them out with more positive thoughts — then we will suffer unnecessarily. Why? Because all those very popular 'common sense' strategies require a huge amount of time and effort and energy, and for most people, they really don't work too well in the long term. Those thoughts may disappear for a while, but like zombies in a horror movie, they soon return.

However, there is an alternative approach that is generally much more helpful. We can learn to separate from our thoughts; to 'detach' or 'unhook' ourselves from them. We can learn to let them come and go, as if they are cars driving past our house. If you're anywhere near a road right now, open your ears and see if you can hear the sounds of traffic. Sometimes there is a lot of traffic outside and sometimes there is very little. But what happens if we try to make the traffic stop? Can we do it? Can we magically wish it away? And what happens if we get angry at the traffic, if we pace up and down, ranting and raving about it? Does this help us live with the traffic? Isn't it easier just to let those cars come and go and invest our energy in something more useful?

And suppose a noisy old car drives slowly past your house, engine roaring, exhaust firing and loud music booming from within. You look out of the window and see the car is covered with rust and graffiti, and there's a group of young lads inside, singing along, whooping it up, shouting obscenities. What is the best thing to do? To run out of the house and start yelling at the car, 'Go away. You have no right to be here?' To patrol up and down the street all night long, to ensure it doesn't come back? To attempt to keep such cars away in future, by asking the universe to provide only beautiful cars outside your house?

The easiest and simplest approach is to just let that car come and go: acknowledge it is present and allow it to pass on through in its own good time. And the same strategy applies to our own thoughts. With a bit of practice, we can learn to acknowledge the thoughts that are present and let them pass on through in their own good time, without getting caught up in them and without any need to challenge them.

This capacity to separate from our thoughts is essential for us to be fully present. I mentioned in the last chapter that in ACT we call this process 'defusion', and the first step is to *notice* that we are absorbed in our thoughts. Now if you've actually tried doing this, you'll have discovered it is not as easy as it sounds. The problem is, our minds are just so good at pulling us into their stories. You know how hard it is to put down a gripping novel, or to press 'pause' when you're halfway through watching a great movie; and all too often our mental stories are every bit as compelling. Indeed, I often liken the mind to a masterful hypnotist who lures us into a trance with clever words. And it can be incredibly hard to break that trance. However, like every new skill, if we practise, we improve — and over time it gets easier, especially when you use the tips in this chapter.

Let's begin with a closer look at that first step: noticing. As we do this, we aim to notice two things simultaneously:

    a) what our mind is doing, and

    b) how we are responding to it.

In other words, we notice what thoughts we are having and we notice to what extent we are fused or defused. It is not like there are two discrete states: that we're either fused or defused. Rather than black and white, there are many shades of grey. We might be very fused or slightly fused. We might be extremely defused or just a little bit defused. Generally speaking, the less impact and influence a thought has over us, the more we are likely to talk of being 'defused'. Conversely, the more impact and influence it has, the more we are likely to talk of being 'fused'.

When you take a moment to notice what your mind is doing and how you are responding to it, it's a bit like pausing the movie on your DVD player; for a moment, you interrupt the story, so you can take stock of your surroundings and do whatever you need to. Unfortunately, this analogy breaks down if we look at it too closely. When we pause a movie, the picture stays static for as long as we wish, but when we pause to notice our mind, the thoughts hold still for only a split second and then the flow of words and pictures resumes. Still, I'm sure you get the point: when we pause the movie, we are no longer '*in* the story'. We can step back from it and see it for what it is: nothing more than sounds and pictures on a screen. And the same thing happens when we pause to notice our mind.

Let's try this now. When you get to the end of this paragraph, put the book down, pause for about thirty seconds, and notice (with curiosity) what your mind does. Does it go silent? Does it generate some new words or pictures? Does it protest: 'This is silly' or 'Nothing's happening!'?

* * *

So, did your mind have something to say, or did it go quiet? If your thoughts stopped, lucky you; thought-free moments are rare, so enjoy them! Far more commonly, when we pause to notice the mind, we discover it is very active. And once we have noticed this activity, the next step in defusion is to *name* it. For example, we could silently say to ourselves 'thinking'. Naming the process of 'thinking' helps us to separate ourselves a little from all those words; to step back and get a bit of distance.

'Thinking' is a good overall term that covers just about every activity the mind does — but at times it's helpful to be a bit more specific. For instance, when we notice we're all caught up in thoughts about things that might go wrong, we could name it 'worrying'. Similarly, if we're going over old grievances or thinking of all the ways others have wronged us, we might name that activity 'blaming' or 'resentment'. If we're lost in fantasies, we might name it 'daydreaming'. If we're going over our problems without reaching any useful outcomes, we might call it 'stewing' or 'ruminating'. If we're reliving painful memories, we might call it 'remembering'.

When we follow noticing with naming, we generally create more distance from our thoughts. Suppose you wake in fright from a bad dream. The first thing you do is notice that you're awake and in your bedroom. The next thing you do is name the experience: 'It was only a dream.' As you do this, you wake up further; the dream becomes more distant, the bedroom more present.

And let's not forget that we don't have to be deadly serious about this. We could name the process in all manner of playful ways. We might say to ourselves, with a sense of humour, 'Oops! Lost in the smog again', or 'Thanks mind, that's an interesting story', or '*That* old movie again'. We might name it 'Storytelling', or 'Story time', or we might say, 'Aha! I've heard this story before'.

When we respond to our thoughts in this manner, we are not concerned as to whether they are true or false. Instead, we ask ourselves, 'Are these thoughts helpful? If I hold on tightly to this story — if I get all caught up in it, or allow it to push me around and dictate what I do — then will that help me to be the person

I want to be, or do the things I want to do? Will it help me adapt to or improve my situation?'

If the answer is 'No', then it makes sense to take a step back and unhook ourselves from the story: to pause, notice and name it. To pay attention and see it for what it is: a sequence of pictures and words passing by.

You can even take 'naming the story' a step further. Imagine you are going to write a book or make a documentary about your current reality gap and you are going to put all your painful thoughts, feelings and memories into it. And you are going to give it a title that begins with the word 'The' and ends with the word 'Story', for example, 'The "My Life Is Over" Story' or 'The "Old and Lonely" Story'. It needs to be a title that:

a) summarises the issue, and

b) acknowledges that this issue has been a huge source of pain in your life.

It can't be a title that trivialises the issue or makes fun of it. It can be a humorous title if you wish, but not a mocking or demeaning or trivialising one. (So if you try this technique and you end up feeling belittled or demeaned or invalidated, then you will need to change the title.) Once you've come up with a title, use it to enhance the naming process: any time a thought, feeling or memory linked to this reality gap arises, notice it and name it. For instance, 'Aha! There it is again: 'The "Underachiever" Story'.

A few years back, a middle-aged psychologist, let's call her Naomi, attended one of my workshops. During the mid-morning tea break she confided in me that she had a malignant brain tumour. She had tried all the conventional medical treatments and many alternative ones as well (such as meditation, prayer, faith healing, creative visualisation, homeopathy, numerous diets and herbal remedies, positive thinking and self-hypnosis) but, sadly, the tumour was incurable and Naomi did not have much longer to live. She was attending my workshop to help herself cope with her fear, and to make the most of whatever life she had left. Naomi told me it was difficult to remain focused in the workshop. She was continually getting hooked by thoughts of death; she kept thinking of her loved ones and how they would react; she kept 'seeing' her MRI scans and that tumour spreading progressively through her brain; and she kept dwelling on the likely progression of her illness, from paralysis to coma, then death.

Now clearly if we have a terminal illness, it's often helpful to think about the implications: to consider what we put in the will, and what sort of funeral we want, and what we wish to say to our loved ones, and what sort of medical care we need to arrange. But if you've gone to a workshop for personal growth, then it's unhelpful to be fused with such thoughts at that time; you will miss out on the workshop. So I listened compassionately to Naomi and, then, after first acknowledging how much pain she was in and empathising with her fear and validating how difficult it was for her, we talked about naming the story. (If I had leaped straight into defusion, chances are, she would have felt upset or invalidated, as if I were trying to 'fix' or 'save' or 'cure' her without truly understanding or caring just how much pain and difficulty she was in.) So Naomi came up with this title: 'The "Scary Death" Story'.

Next, I asked her to practise naming that story whenever she saw it coming, or whenever she became aware it had hooked her. She did this enthusiastically, and by lunchtime on day two of the workshop she was defused from all those morbid thoughts. The thoughts had not altered in believability — she still considered them all to be true — but she was now able to let them come and go like passing cars, and remain engaged in the workshop.

Noticing and naming our thoughts is usually enough to

break their grip on us, but not always; sometimes we need to add in a third step of defusion, which I call 'neutralising'. Basically this involves doing something to our thoughts to 'neutralise' their power; something that helps us to see their true nature and recognise that they really are nothing more or less than words and pictures. Neutralisation techniques include silently singing your thoughts to popular tunes, saying them to yourself in different voices, drawing them in thought bubbles, visualising them on computer screens, imagining them coming from cartoon characters or historical figures, and more. In Appendix 1, you'll find a number of these exercises, so if you feel like you need more help with defusion, please go there before reading on.

We can't stop that voice in our head from telling us stories, but we can learn to catch it in the act. And we can learn to choose the way we respond: to let the helpful stories guide us, and the unhelpful ones come and go like leaves in the breeze.

Chapter 7

LIVE AND LET GO

Throughout history, humans have made a strong connection between breathing and spirituality. For example, the words 'spirit' and 'inspire' are derived from the Latin word *spiritus*, which has two meanings: 'soul' and 'breath'. Similarly, in Hebrew, the word *ruah* most commonly means 'breath' or 'wind', but it also means 'soul'. Likewise, the Greek word *psyche*, from which we derive terms such as 'psychology' and 'psychiatry', variously means 'soul', 'spirit', 'mind' or 'breath'.

In the Old Testament of the Bible, God formed man from the dust of the ground and breathed life into him through the nostrils. In ancient Greek mythology, man was created out of mud by the God Prometheus, then the Goddess Athene breathed life into him. And in the 'contemplative' or 'mystical' branches of all the world's most popular religions — Christianity, Islam, Buddhism, Hinduism, Sikhism, Judaism and Taoism — there are breathing exercises designed to help one access a higher state of awareness, or a direct experience of the divine.

So how do we explain this strong connection between breath and spirituality? There are many contributing factors. First and foremost is the obvious link between breathing and life. As long as you're breathing, you're alive — which means there is always something purposeful you can do. Another factor is that breathing exercises are often quite soothing or relaxing. They can help us to access a sense of inner peace; to find a safe, calm place in the midst of an emotional storm. A third factor is that we can use our breath to anchor ourselves in the present. When we're all caught up in our thoughts and feelings, we can focus on our breath to ground ourselves and reconnect with our here-and-now experience.

Yet a fourth factor is that breathing can serve as a metaphor for 'letting go'. Our breath flows in and out all day long, and most of the time, we don't try to control it; we let it come and go as it pleases. But, if for some reason we try to hold it in, we find we can't do so for very long. When we hold our breath in, the tension rapidly builds; the internal pressure increases and all manner of unpleasant feelings arise in our body. And then, when we let it go again, the sense of release is instant and profound.

In later chapters, we will explore all of these factors and more but, for now, we'll focus on the breath and letting go. I'm going to invite you to try a little exercise. You may be able to do it while still reading, or you may need to read the instructions first and then put the book down to do it.

Take A Breath, Hold and Let Go

Slowly take a large breath in and once your lungs are filled with air, hold your breath.

Hold the breath for as long as you possibly can.

Notice how, as you keep the breath trapped inside your body, the pressure steadily builds.

Notice what happens in your chest, neck and abdomen.

Notice the tension building and the pressure rising.

Notice the changing feelings in your head, neck, shoulders, chest and abdomen.

And hold that breath.

Keep holding.

Notice how the sensations grow stronger and more unpleasant; how your body tries ever more forcefully to make you exhale.

Observe those physical sensations as if you are a curious child, who has never encountered anything like this before.

And when you can't hold your breath a moment longer, slowly and, ever so gently, release it.

And as you let it go, savour the experience.

Appreciate the simple pleasure of breathing out.

Notice the letting go.

Notice the release of tension.

Notice your lungs deflating and your shoulders dropping.

Appreciate the simple pleasure of letting go.

* * *

How did you find that experience? Were you able to appreciate it? Did you notice a sense of grounding or centring yourself? Perhaps a sense of calmness or stillness?

How often in our day-to-day existence do we hold on to things, refusing stubbornly to let go? We hold on to old hurts, grudges and grievances. We hold on to unhelpful attitudes and prejudices. We hold on to notions of blame and unfairness. We hold on to self-limiting beliefs, old failures and painful memories. We hold on to unrealistic expectations of ourselves, the world or others. We hold on to stories of 'right' and 'wrong' and 'fair' and 'unfair', that pull us into fruitless struggles with reality.

So what if we could get better at 'letting go'? What if we could loosen our grip and stop holding on so tightly? What if we could catch ourselves in the act of holding on to anxiety, frustration, criticism, judgement, resentment or blame and use our breath to remind us to 'let it go'? What difference might that make to our relationships, our health and our vitality?

I now invite you to try another exercise, a little easier than the last one.

Take A Breath, Count To Three

Take a deep breath and hold it for a count of three.
Let the breath leave your lungs as slowly as
   possible.
As you breathe out, let your shoulders drop and feel
   your shoulder blades sliding down your back.
Once again notice the sense of release.
Appreciate the simple pleasure of exhaling.
Notice what it's like to let . . . it . . . go.

I encourage you to try this exercise regularly throughout the day and see what difference it makes. Try it when you are holding on tightly to something — some hurt, resentment or blame that is draining away your vitality. Just breathe, hold and exhale. Many people also find it helpful to silently say something like, 'Letting go'.

Suppose you're stewing over that fight you had with your partner, or replaying the unkind comments your boss made at work, or giving yourself a guilt trip about the way you lost your temper with the kids, or dwelling on how unfairly life has treated you. These are all forms of 'holding on tightly'. And you don't need me to tell you that it doesn't help; that it merely increases your stress and drains your vitality. So once you have caught yourself holding on, the next step is really very simple: take a deep breath, hold it for three and then, very slowly, let . . . it . . . go.

Chapter 8

THE THIRD WAY

While I was writing this chapter; on board a plane, a curious thing happened. The man behind me asked me to put my seat forward because he was trying to write on his laptop computer and my seat was cramping his space. I explained to him that I was sorry for the inconvenience, but I had put my seat backwards to give *me* more room to write on my own computer and I politely suggested he might like to do the same. He didn't like that idea and asked me again to move my seat forward. I noticed he had an empty seat next to him and suggested he might like to sit there. 'No thanks,' he said, 'I want to sit by the window.' I replied, 'Well, I'm sorry, but I want to sit with my seat back and I do have the right to do so.' He was furious about this and said, 'Right then, well, I'll just have to make myself comfortable, won't I?' and he forcefully banged his knees into the back of my seat. I pondered what to do; he was bigger, younger, stronger and tougher than me and I didn't want to aggravate him. On the other hand, I didn't want to let him bully me into putting my seat upright either. So I thought to myself, *I'll just ride this out for a few minutes; after all, it's probably far more uncomfortable for him, pounding his knees into the chair, than it is for me on the other side, and if he doesn't settle down, I'll call the flight attendant.* So I shifted in my chair, found a position in which his blows had minimal effect, and started typing away on my computer.

For the first minute or so, his pounding was quite annoying, but as I got absorbed in my writing, it faded into the background and, as I had expected, over the space of a few minutes, he settled down. Still, every five minutes or so, he'd bang the back of my seat a few times, just to let me know he was still angry. And because the chair beside him was empty, and he was careful as to when he made his moves, the flight attendants didn't notice, and nor did the other passengers (I assume).

As time went on, I began to find these outbursts quite amusing. At first my amusement stemmed from an attitude of 'holier than thou'; I was looking down at him, as if I was somehow superior. I thought of him as a spoilt brat having a tantrum because he can't get his own way. But after a while, I let go of my smugness as I recognised that I, too, often have my own tantrums, and while I never resort to physical aggression, there are plenty of times that I have snapped or yelled at my loved ones, or sulked and fretted when I didn't get my own way. I remember how furious I was when my son was diagnosed with autism; how I raged against reality. And sometimes when I couldn't contain it any longer, I took out all that pent-up anger on my wife — criticising her, judging her and blaming her (as if she didn't have enough to cope with already; as if she wasn't hurting just as much as I was).

Don't we all have these temper tantrums at times? It's easy for us to judge others as being childish or spoilt or overly aggressive, but truth be told, there's a little child inside all of us who really wants to have his or her own way, and acts childishly when he or she doesn't get it.

After this insight, I reflected on how unpleasant it is to be caught up in anger or frustration and how uncomfortable we often feel later — guilty, embarrassed or even angry *at ourselves* — once we realise how badly we have behaved. And at that point, I started to feel compassion for this man behind me. Clearly he was suffering and clearly the situation was hurting him a lot more than me.

The intermittent bursts of knee-knocking continued for about twenty minutes before they finally stopped. And then, about ten minutes later, something wonderful happened. The man behind me stuck his head over the back of my seat and said, 'I'm really sorry, mate. I don't know what I was doing.' His anger had completely melted and his face had a lovely, warm softness to it. 'I'm so embarrassed. I've just had a shit of a day and I took it out on you. I'm really sorry.' Then he stuck his hand through the gap between our seats, offering a handshake.

'No worries, mate,' I said, clasping his hand warmly. 'I'm actually grateful to you.'

'What do you mean?' he asked.

'Well, I was just writing about you in a book that's going to be published in a few months' time — and now you've given me a lovely ending to the story.'

'Mate,' he said, his face beaming, 'that's great. That makes my heart swell.'

Wouldn't it be great if these sorts of incidents always had such good outcomes? Obviously this man had been totally lost in the smog; note his words: *'I don't know what I was doing.'* However, when he eventually got present, he was big enough to acknowledge his error and make amends. Unfortunately, in everyday life, it often doesn't turn out so positively. And this is in large part because we grow up in a society that doesn't teach us how to handle strong emotions effectively. Most of us, by the time we reach adulthood, know only two ways of dealing with painful feelings: control or be controlled.

Control or Be Controlled

As infants, toddlers and young children, we are largely controlled by our feelings. Fear, anger, sadness, guilt, frustration and anxiety: these emotions, and many others, push children around as if they are remote-controlled robots. If anger shows up, they shout or yell or lash out, or stomp their feet. If fear shows up, they hide or cry or run away. If sadness or disappointment shows up, they sulk or cry or bawl.

Fortunately, as adults, we are much less controlled by our feelings, and this is a good thing. We would all be in big trouble if our feelings controlled us. Imagine if you were at the mercy of your fear, anger, sadness and guilt; if it pushed you around exactly as it did when you were a child. How difficult would life be for you?

Of course, just like that man on the plane, we all allow our emotions to control us at times. We may lose our temper, get carried away by our fears, find ourselves overwhelmed with sadness, get crushed with guilt, or go into a fit of blind rage. But fortunately, this happens much less than it did in childhood (at least, for most people). And this is because, as we grew older, we learned all sorts of ways to control our feelings.

For example, we learned how to distract ourselves from unpleasant emotions via food, music, TV, books or games. And as we grew older still, the potential distractions multiplied: exercise, work, study, hobbies, religion, computer games, email, gambling, sex, pornography, music, sport, drugs, alcohol, gardening, walking the dog, cooking, dancing and so on.

We also learned how to escape unpleasant feelings by avoiding the situations where they were most likely to occur. In other words, we learned to withdraw or stay away from the people, places, activities or tasks we found difficult or challenging.

Then there are all those thinking strategies we developed

that, at times, could give us some relief from emotional pain. You probably have dozens of these strategies, such as:
- constructive problem solving
- writing lists
- looking at the situation from a different perspective
- blaming or criticising others
- vigorously defending your position
- positive affirmations
- telling yourself inspirational quotes such as, 'This shall pass' or 'What does not hurt me makes me stronger'
- trivialising the issue or pretending it's not important
- comparing yourself to others who are worse off.

And last but not least, we have all discovered that putting substances into our bodies — whether it be chocolate, ice-cream, pizza, toast, tea, coffee, drugs, alcohol, tobacco, herbal remedies or prescription medication — often only gives temporary relief from painful feelings.

And yet, even with all these clever ways to control our feelings, we continue to suffer psychologically. We are not free from emotional pain for long. Think of the happiest day of your life; how long did those joyous, happy feelings last before some anxiety, frustration, disappointment or irritation show up?

The fact is that to live a full human life is to experience the full range of human emotions — not just the ones that 'feel good'. Our feelings are like the weather, continually changing: at times very pleasant, at other times extremely uncomfortable. And what would happen if we went through life believing, *'We should have good weather every day. There must be something seriously wrong if it's cold and wet outside.'* If this was our attitude, how much would we struggle with reality? How much would our life shrink if we believed, *'I can't do the things that really matter to me, or be the person I want to be, unless the weather is good*'?

When we talk about the weather this way it seems ridiculous. We know we can't control the weather, so we don't even try to. We let the weather do what it does and we change our clothes to adapt. But when it comes to emotions, most of us do the opposite; we try as hard as we can to get control of them, and this is quite natural. After all, everyone wants to feel good, and no one wants to feel bad. So we try to push our unwanted feelings away with quick fixes of 'feel good' activities, and this is reinforced by all the people out there who claim they can help us: *Buy a new car! Go on a holiday! Whiten your teeth! Have a Botox injection! Drink our excellent bourbon! Try our delicious new ice-cream! Buy our product and you too can be as happy as the young, fit, healthy, beautiful, slim, sun-tanned, smiling person in this advert.* And, of course, many of these things do give us pleasant feelings, but how long do they last? A few minutes? Perhaps a few hours?

As we journey through life, we all experience intense and uncomfortable emotions that we can't simply turn off at the flick of a switch. And you've undoubtedly discovered that often the strategies we use to control our emotions tend to impair our quality of life in the long term. This is most obvious when it comes to things such as drugs, alcohol, tobacco, chocolate and gambling, but if you look closely, with an open mind, you'll find it applies to any control strategy that we use *excessively* or *rigidly*.

Even something as healthy as exercise will become problematic if we use it *excessively* or *rigidly* to try to control our feelings. For example, some people suffering from anorexia exercise vigorously every day and, in the short term, this helps them to control their feelings of anxiety — to push away all those fears about getting fat — but in the long term, it keeps their bodies in a state of extremely unhealthy thinness. This is obviously very different from exercising *flexibly* and being guided by core values about looking after your health and wellbeing.

Often, the disappointments and setbacks we encounter when we attempt to control our emotions just spur us on to try even harder, to find even cleverer ways to control how we feel. The hope is that one day we will find the ultimate strategy; one that will give us excellent control of our feelings. But sooner or later, we realise this is a lost cause. To emphasise this point, whenever I give workshops or lectures, I ask all the parents in the room to raise their hands. Usually, this is well over three-quarters of the audience. I say, 'Having a child enriches your life enormously and gives you some of the most wonderful feelings you will ever have — love, joy and tenderness, the likes of which you could never have imagined. But are those the only feelings that children give you?'

Everyone shakes their heads and says, 'Nooooo!'

'What other feelings do children give you?' I ask.

There is a cacophony of responses: fear, anger, exhaustion, worry, guilt, sadness, pain, frustration, rejection, boredom and rage to name a few.

And there you have it: the things that make life rich, full and meaningful give rise to a wide range of feelings — not just 'good' ones. (This, of course, holds true for every loving relationship, not just those with our children. No wonder the philosopher Jean-Paul Sartre said, 'Hell is other people'.)

Unfortunately, this realisation can take a long time to come. It may take us a hundred self-help books, or twenty years of therapy, or five different types of prescription medication, or a dozen self-empowerment courses, or decades of silent struggle, or a lifetime of seeking advice from various 'experts' before we truly realise the simple truth: when it comes to painful emotions, we have not been well educated by our society. We have grown up learning only two ways of responding: control or be controlled. And if these are our only two options, will we ever find inner fulfilment?

Sometimes I have clients who react quite negatively to these ideas; they were clinging to the idea that fulfilment means no more painful feelings. *If only!* Fulfilment does not mean our difficult emotions disappear; it means we change our relationship with them. We find a new way of responding to them, so that when they arise, they can't hold us back from being present, living with purpose and experiencing life as a privilege. We learn how to access a state of peacefulness and stillness in the midst of our pain; how to 'create a space' within ourselves through which our feelings can freely flow without pushing us around or bringing us down. I call this ability 'expansion': one of the three core skills involved in presence.

Now before we go any further, time for a confession. When I first heard that dreadful word 'autism' applied to my son, I forgot just about everything I've written in this chapter. I tried desperately to run away from my pain. I tried frantically to distract myself with books, music, DVDs, television and the Internet. But it didn't work. Thoughts about my son would continually creep up and drag me away; dark stories full of stark, gloomy images: my little boy impaired, disabled, rejected — an outcast of society.

I also tried to escape through my favourite comfort food: double-coated chocolate Tim Tams. But this didn't work either. I'd get a few moments of relief while the food was in my mouth, but as soon as it was gone, the pain would be back with a vengeance (and I gained several kilograms in the process!).

I tried to escape through being proactive. I hit the Internet with a vengeance, reading everything I could find about autism and its treatment, trying to sort the science from the nonsense.

But that didn't help either. Nor did talking about it with friends, or drinking alcohol, or bawling my eyes out, or going for long walks, or having a massage, or thinking positively, or repeating inspiring quotes.

At times like these, when the reality gap is enormous, there is no way to control our pain to make it go away (unless you turn to something so drastic, like the heavy use of drugs and alcohol, that it will seriously impair your life in the long term and open lots of other reality gaps). If we allow our pain to control us it will only make everything so much harder. So our only sensible choice is to practise expansion.

Expansion

'Expansion' is radically different to the first two approaches: 'control' and 'be controlled'. However, because it is so radically different, it often takes a while to understand it. So, to get a sense of what the 'third way' involves, carry out the following experiment.

A Four-step Experiment

There are four steps to this experiment, and you will get much more out of it if you actually *do* it, rather than simply reading about it.

STEP 1: Imagine that the book in your hands is made up of all the emotions that you find most difficult to handle. (Take a few moments to name them.)

STEP 2: When you reach the end of this paragraph,

hold this book around the edges, while keeping it open at the centre. Gripping the edges tightly, lift the open book up in front of your face, then bring it in so close that it's almost touching your nose — the book should be virtually wrapped around your face, completely obscuring your view of your surroundings. Hold it like that for about twenty seconds and notice what the experience is like.

What did you discover? While you were totally 'caught up in your emotions', did you feel a bit lost, disoriented or cut off from the world around you? Did it seem as if your emotions dominated everything? Did your view of the room disappear? Were you 'consumed' by the experience?

This is what it is like when we are controlled by our emotions: we get caught up in them, lost in them and overwhelmed by them. They dominate our experience. We wallow in them, get 'held back', or let them push us around. It is hard to be present, or respond effectively to the many difficult challenges of life, when we react to our emotions in this way.

STEP 3: Once again, imagine that this book contains all your most difficult emotions. When you reach the end of this paragraph, take the book in both hands, grip it tightly around the edges, and hold it as far away from you as you possibly can. Push your arms out as far as you possibly can (without actually dislocating your shoulders!), straighten them fully at the elbows, and keep the book at arm's length. Hold it like that for about one minute and notice what the experience is like.

Did you find that uncomfortable or tiring? Imagine doing this all day long; how exhausting would it be? And imagine watching your favourite movie or TV show, or having a conversation, or eating a meal, or making love at the same time as doing this exercise. How much would it distract you or interfere with your enjoyment? This is what it is like when we try to control our emotions: we exert a huge amount of energy into pushing them away. Not only is this draining and distracting; it also pulls us out of the here-and-now and into an internal struggle. When we are trying hard to control our emotions, it is very difficult to be present and respond effectively to life's challenges.

STEP 4: When you reach the end of this paragraph (again pretending this book holds all your most painful feelings), place the book gently on your lap and let it sit there for twenty seconds. And as you let it sit there, stretch your arms, breathe deeply, and with childlike curiosity scan your surroundings, and notice what you can see, hear and smell.

This is the third way of responding to painful emotions: making room for them or 'expansion'. (Note: the official term in ACT is not 'expansion' but 'acceptance'. I tend to avoid the word 'acceptance' because most people misunderstand it: they either think it means liking, wanting, or approving of your emotions; or tolerating, putting up with, or resigning yourself to them.) 'Expansion' means opening up and creating space for our emotions; letting them come and stay and go in their own good time, as and when they choose, without investing any energy in struggling with them or hiding from them. Did you notice how letting the book sit on your lap was so much easier, so much less distracting and so much less effort, than getting caught up in it or keeping it at arm's length? Did you notice that when you disentangled yourself from it, stopped struggling with it and made space for it, you could be fully present with the world around you?

Sometimes when I take my clients through this exercise they say, 'Yes, but that's just a book. It's not that easy with real emotions.'

I reply, 'You are absolutely right. This is merely an exercise.'

And the point of this exercise is to prepare you for where we go next: doing expansion for real.

Chapter 9

A CURIOUS LOOK

A wave of nausea washes over you. Your eyesight becomes blurry and foggy, and within a few seconds, it completely disappears. Your throat is paralysed almost instantly, preventing you from speaking or swallowing. And over the next two to three minutes, this paralysis spreads throughout your body, until you can no longer breathe. This is how your life would end if you were bitten by the tiny bird-like beak of the deadly blue-ringed octopus, an organism no bigger than a tennis ball.

A good friend of mine, Paddy Spruce, likes to ask the question, 'If you were swimming near a blue-ringed octopus, would you pick it up, chase it away, ignore it or simply observe it?' Clearly all these options are available to us, but the first two are deadly, and while this octopus is not naturally aggressive, if you try to pick it up or threaten it in any way, it will bite. (Just before it attacks, you will see the blue rings on its tentacles suddenly light up.) As for the third option — ignoring it — that would be pretty hard to do, knowing how deadly it is. Plus, if you don't pay attention to where it is, you might accidentally swim into it.

So the last option, observing it, is clearly the best. 'Hang on a minute,' you might be thinking, 'there's another option you didn't mention. I could swim away from it.' Yes, you could.

However, the blue-ringed octopus prefers to hide under rocks rather than swim in the open, so if you stay still and observe, it will soon pass on by and leave you alone. And even if you choose to swim away, wouldn't you first want to get a good look at it, knowing that as long as you don't try to pick it up or threaten it, you are perfectly safe?

This tiny sea creature provides a good analogy for a painful emotion; if you hold on to it, chase it away, or try to ignore it, the results are usually bad. Unfortunately, many of us treat our emotions as if they are as dangerous as that octopus. We want to get rid of them or avoid them. We can't be at ease when they're around. We try to figure out how to make them go away. And this attitude, unfortunately, absorbs a lot of our energy and drains our vitality. However, it doesn't have to be that way. Why? Because unlike the octopus, our feelings are *not* dangerous. If we stay still and observe our emotions with curiosity, then they cannot hurt us or harm us in any way; and like that blue-ringed octopus, sooner or later they will pass.

Now suppose you were a marine biologist and you had paid a small fortune for the opportunity to observe the blue-ringed octopus in its natural environment. Under those circumstances, knowing you were safe, you'd observe that creature with absolute fascination. You'd be curious about its every move. You'd notice the rhythmic movements of its tentacles; you'd notice the beautiful patterns and colours on its body; and you'd respect it as a magnificent work of nature. In other words, you'd be fully present. And it's this type of open, curious attention that comprises the basis of expansion.

And if that sounds at all familiar to you, it should, because expansion is an aspect of presence. In other words, when a painful feeling arises, you don't have to get sucked into it and you don't need to try to get away from it; instead, you can be fully present with it. And if your mind has something unhelpful to say about that prospect — a protest, threat, worry, judgement, or some other form of resistance — then please let it have its say and carry on reading.

Thoughts, Feelings, Emotions and Sensations

As many people get confused about the differences between thoughts, feelings, emotions and sensations, it's worth taking a moment to clarify them. However, this task is slightly tricky because most 'experts' can't completely agree on what an emotion actually is. But there are some things they do agree on. For example, there's no doubt that emotions prepare us for action. Sadness, anger, fear, guilt, love and joy all predispose us to behave in particular ways. Also, on a physical level, an emotion includes neurological changes (i.e. involving the brain and nervous system), cardiovascular changes (i.e. involving the heart and circulatory system), and hormonal changes (i.e. involving the 'chemical messengers' of the blood).

However, while we can measure these changes on scientific instruments, this is not how we experience our own emotions.

When we look at our emotions with open, curious attention, all we will ever encounter are thoughts and sensations. By 'thoughts', I mean words and pictures inside our head; by 'sensations', I mean what we feel inside our body. As for 'feelings', some people use this word interchangeably with 'emotions' (as I do throughout this book), but others use it to mean the physical sensations that arise as part of an emotion (as opposed to the thoughts that are also part of the emotion).

The best way to make sense of this is to check it out for yourself: observe your emotions with curiosity. As you do this, you will either notice something comprised of sensations or something comprised of words and pictures. Or rather, you will notice complex, interweaving, multilayered tapestries of pictures, words and sensations. And you can zoom in on specific thoughts or sensations, or you can zoom out and take in the whole spectacle.

Often emotions give rise to a sense of meaning, but that 'meaning' itself is a thought, made of words and pictures. Urges also often show up as part of a strong emotion; but pay close attention to any urge, and what you will discover are sensations in your body, and words and pictures in your head. The same also holds true for any memories: look at the memory closely and again you will discover sensations in your body, and words and pictures in your head. (And if your memory involves smell or taste, well, those are also sensations.)

To make this clearer, consider your favourite movie. If you were to watch a one-second segment of that film, all you would encounter are sounds and pictures. We wouldn't call any one of those sounds or pictures a movie in itself; and we wouldn't say a movie is nothing but 'sounds and pictures'. But, *experientially*, when you look at any second of any movie, all you will encounter are sounds and pictures. You can think of an emotion similarly: a rich, compelling, multilayered creation comprised of many, many interweaving sensations and thoughts.

Recently I discussed this concept in an email exchange. My correspondent wrote back, 'I see what you're saying . . . and yet . . . there's something else in an emotion that can perhaps only be described as like a flavour or a colour . . . amorphous, but at the same time sharp! Perhaps it's a spiky, colourful, amorphous blob!'

I replied, 'The thing is, a flavour is a sensation — a sensation of taste. It may seem amorphous (i.e. it has no clear shape) but you can sense where it is located in your body through noticing the sensations of pressure, temperature, pulsation, etc. If you experience a colour, then you must be 'seeing' a picture of some sort (even if it is an abstract picture — pure colour with no obvious shape). If you experience it as 'sharp' or 'spiky', you either have encountered a sensation of sharpness or you have imagined a picture of something sharp. So when you zoom in and observe any aspect of that 'spiky, colourful, amorphous blob' you will find sensations, words and pictures. And then the question is, can you open up and make room for whatever you encounter?'

When we pay attention to the threatening, unpleasant or painful stuff inside us — to all those thoughts and feelings that we normally turn away from — and when we are willing to take a good honest look at it all and really examine it with openness and curiosity, then we are likely to discover something useful. We learn that it is not as big as it seems; that we can make room for it. We learn that it cannot harm us, even though it feels unpleasant. We learn that it cannot control our arms and legs, even though it may make us shiver and shake. We learn that there is no need to run and hide from it, nor to fight and struggle with it. This frees us up to invest time and energy in improving our life, rather than in trying to control the way we feel. Without genuine curiosity, it is unlikely we will ever discover this.

Normally, when painful feelings arise, we are not curious about them. We have no desire to get up close and study them and see what they are comprised of. We have no particular interest in learning from them. Generally speaking, we don't want to know about them at all. We want to forget about them, distract ourselves from them, or get rid of them as fast as possible. Rather than take a close look at them, we instinctively turn away. It is much the same as the way we automatically recoil or avert our gaze from the sight of a diseased or deformed body. And yet, as automatic as it is, this is a response that we can change with practice.

Working as a doctor, I have had the opportunity to see many different ways in which the human body can become deformed: through blistering skin diseases, the terrible scarring of burns, the merciless rampages of cancer and AIDS, the distorted swollen joints of immune disorders, the missing limbs that result from surgical amputations, the misshapen heads and twisted spines of rare genetic disorders, the bloated abdomens and yellowing flesh of liver disease, and the myriad forms of physical deterioration associated with old age, illness and death.

Before I entered the medical profession, I felt a sense of shock, fear, aversion or disgust whenever I saw people with these conditions. But over the years, I gradually learned to see past the unpleasant exterior and connect with the human being inside. I learned to pay attention with warmth, curiosity and openness and, over time, my aversion and fear disappeared and in its place came kindness and compassion. However, this only happened through my willingness to be present and open up; to make room for my automatic emotional reactions, without letting them control me. If we are willing, we are all capable of making this transition.

At this point, let's note that there are two very different types of curiosity. There is a cold, detached, uncaring curiosity, such as that of a lab scientist doing experiments on a rat or monkey. And then there is a warm, caring curiosity, such as that of a kindly vet trying to work out how to heal a sick animal. You've probably met some doctors who are cold and detached, curious only about the illness, interested only in the diagnosis and treatment. They seem to care very little about the human being inside that afflicted body. And you've probably met other doctors who are the opposite: warm, kind and caring in their curiosity. They care first and foremost about the human being; they treat the whole person, not just the condition. Which kind of doctor would you prefer to have treating you?

The word 'curiosity' originates from the Latin term *curiosus*, which means 'careful' or 'diligent'. This, in turn, comes from the Latin word *cura*, which means 'care'. I find this very interesting. When practising mindfulness, we are caring for ourselves; we care about what we feel and we care about how we respond to our feelings. Avoidance of our feelings is, in contrast, very often an uncaring act. We get so focused on trying any way possible to get rid of them that we end up harming ourselves or shrinking our lives in the process. The word *cura* also gives us the word 'cure' and this seems appropriate because curiosity plays such an essential role in emotional healing; instead of trying to escape from our pain, we turn towards it, investigate it, explore it and, ultimately, make room for it. This is a true act of caring and healing.

So next time loneliness, resentment, anxiety, guilt, sadness, regret or fear shows up, what if you could become really curious about those experiences? What if you could shine a light on them, study them as if they were the prize exhibit in a show?

As we look more curiously into any intense stress or discomfort, we will find that it is comprised of two major components. One is the storyline: a bunch of words and pictures inside our head — beliefs, ideas, assumptions, reasons, rules, judgements, impressions, interpretations, images and memories. The other is our body sense: all the different feelings and sensations inside our body. And as we've already dealt with stories, we are now going to focus on the sensations.

Sensations

In order to understand the power of sensations, bring to mind a difficult emotion by thinking about your current reality gap. Once you've tapped into some pain, work step-by-step through the exercises that follow. (And if you want a voice to guide you through this process, you can purchase my MP3 *The Reality Slap* from www.thehappinesstrap.com, which contains recordings for all the exercises in this book.)

Notice Your Emotion

Pause for a moment.

You are about to embark on a voyage of discovery; to explore your painful emotion and see it with new eyes.

Take a slow, deep breath and focus your attention on your body.

Start at the top of your head and scan downwards. Notice where in your body this feeling is strongest: your forehead, eyes, jaw, mouth, throat, neck, shoulders, chest, abdomen, pelvis, buttocks, arms or legs? (If you have gone numb, continue with the exercise, but focus on the sensations of the numbness.)

Once you have located this feeling, observe it with wide-eyed curiosity, as if you are a marine biologist who has encountered some fascinating new denizen of the deep. See if you can discover something new about it — about where it is, what it feels like, or how it behaves.

Notice its energy, pulsation or vibration.

Notice the different 'layers' within it.

Notice where it starts and stops.

Is it deep or shallow? Moving or still? Light or heavy?

What is its temperature? Can you notice hot spots or cold spots within it?

Notice any resistance you may have to it. Is your body tensing up around it? Are you breathing more rapidly and shallowly? Is your mind protesting or fretting?

Name Your Emotion

As you notice your emotion, name it. Silently say to yourself, 'Here's fear' or 'Here's anger' or 'Here's guilt'. (If you can't pinpoint the exact name of the emotion, then try: 'Here's pain', or 'Here's stress' or 'Here's numbness'.)

And continue to observe this emotion, as if it is some fascinating sea creature. The big difference now is this creature has a name; you know what you are dealing with.

Breathe Into Your Emotion

Breathe slowly and deeply, and imagine your breath flowing into and around the emotion.

And as your breath does this, it's as if in some way you expand — as if a space opens up inside you.

This is the space of awareness.

And just as the ocean has room for all its inhabitants, your own spacious awareness can easily contain all your emotions.

So breathe into the feeling and open around it.

Loosen up around it. Give it space.

Breathe into any resistance within your body: the tension, the knots, the contraction; and make space for all of that too.

Breathe into any resistance from your mind: the
smoky haze of 'No' or 'Bad' or 'Go away'.

And as you release the breath, also release your
thoughts. Instead of holding on to them, let them
come and go like leaves in the breeze.

Allow Your Emotion

There is no need to like, want or approve of this
emotion. Just see if you can allow it.

Allow it to be where it is. It's already there, so why
fight it?

Make peace with it.

Let it have its space.

Give it room to move.

Give it permission to do what it's already doing; to
be as it already is.

Expand Your Presence

The marine biologist may concentrate her attention
on the octopus, but she can also broaden her
focus, to notice the water around it and the rocks
beneath it.

And we can all widen our focus in a similar way.
Thus, once you've made space for your feeling, the
aim is to expand your awareness. Continue to
notice your feeling and, at the same time,
recognise it is only one aspect of the here and
now.

Around this feeling is your body, and with that
body you can see, hear, touch, taste and smell.

So take a step back and admire the view; do not only notice what you are feeling, but also what you are hearing, seeing and touching.

Think of your awareness as the beam of a powerful torch, revealing what lies hidden in the darkness. Shine it in all directions, to get a clear sense of where you are.

As you do this, do not try to distract yourself from this feeling. And do not try to ignore it. Keep it in your awareness, while at the same time, connecting with the world around you.

Allow the feeling to be there, along with everything else that is also present.

Notice what you are feeling and thinking.

Notice what you are doing and how you are breathing.

Notice it all. Take it all in.

Straddle two worlds with your awareness: the one within you and the one outside you. Illuminate both with your consciousness.

And engage fully in life as it is in this moment.

* * *

As with all mindfulness exercises, the one above can be practised at any time and in any place for any duration. For example, if you want to develop your ability at expansion, you could stretch it into a long exercise, taking a good ten to fifteen minutes. On the other hand, you can practise a ten- to fifteen-second version just about anywhere: simply notice and name the emotion, breathe into it, allow it to be there, and expand your awareness to connect with the world around you.

Now perhaps you may be wondering, '*What's next? After*

I expand my awareness and engage with the world around me, then what do I do?' The answer is, if you're doing something purposeful and life-enhancing, keep doing it and engage in it fully; focus all your attention on the task at hand and become thoroughly absorbed in it. And if you're *not* doing something purposeful and life-enhancing, then stop what you're doing and switch to an activity that is more meaningful. (And if you can't think of any meaningful activities, don't worry, we'll get to that in Part 4: Take A Stand.)

At this point, I need to give you an important reminder: you don't have to stop using all your control strategies (i.e. the things you do to try to control your emotions). Control strategies are only problematic when you use them excessively, or over-rely on them, or when they give you relief from pain in the short term but impair your quality of life in the long term. The point is to enlarge your toolkit so you have more options than just 'control or be controlled'.

So I encourage you to make the effort, at least several times a day, to take a good curious look at your feelings. And if you find this difficult to do, then take baby steps. No one expects a fire fighter to tackle a towering inferno without any training. The trainee fire fighter practises on small, safe fires, lit under carefully controlled conditions within specially designed training grounds. And it is much the same when it comes to mindfulness of our emotions. If you've never tried this approach before, don't begin with your most overwhelming emotions. Start with those smaller, less challenging feelings: the hundred different forms of impatience, frustration, disappointment and anxiety that arise as part of everyday living.

Watch your emotions closely and discover their habits. When do they appear? What brings them out? Which parts of your body do they like to occupy? And how does your body react to them? Where do you notice the resistance, the tension and the struggle?

When watching a documentary, we can be thrilled at the sight of a shark or a crocodile or a stingray. These deadly, vicious creatures can fill us with awe and appreciation. Our challenge is to view our emotions in much the same way. For, although our feelings may appear to be dangerous, they are actually unable to harm us in any way. Unlike a shark or a crocodile, they cannot eat us. Unlike a stingray, they cannot poison us. Watching our feelings mindfully is no more dangerous than watching a wildlife documentary. So take a curious look, whenever you can. It doesn't have to be a long look, just a curious one.

Chapter 10

TAKE OFF YOUR GOGGLES

There are three simple words that can instantly create a reality gap in any area of life in any moment. They are: *not good enough*. All our mind needs to do is judge someone or something as *not good enough* and immediately we are dissatisfied. At times our minds slap these judgements upon ourselves: we are not smart enough, not attractive enough, not successful enough, not a good enough parent or partner or friend. At times our minds slap these judgements on someone we know: he or she is not honest enough, not kind enough, or not interesting enough. And at times our minds slap these judgements on just about anything: our thighs, our house, our achievements, our income, the weather, the neighbourhood, the in-laws, our kids' behaviour, our dog's behaviour, our own behaviour; in some way or other it's just *not good enough*.

And if we buy into this story, as we readily do, it instantly pulls us into a struggle with whatever is on the other side of that judgement. To become dissatisfied with our job, or disappointed in our friends, or unhappy with our body, all we need do is hold on to those three words: *not good enough*. Of course, our mind may not use precisely those words; it might say that our job is 'boring', or our friends are 'unreliable', or our body is 'fat', or our progress is 'too slow', or we are an 'underachiever'. But these judgements all boil down to the same three words: *not good enough*. And while we are lost in this story, fulfilment is impossible; as long as we hold tightly to these words, our discontentment is assured.

Even if our negative judgements are totally justified and we can back them up with all sorts of evidence, the fact is that labelling things as *not good enough* will rarely help us. Usually, all it does is create a reality gap, or enlarge one that is already there!

Now notice your mind's reaction to what I'm saying here: is it with me or against me, sceptical or curious? I want to make something clear: I'm not suggesting that we should just *put up with* the difficult or painful things in life. Nor am I suggesting that we give up on pursuing our goals or getting our needs met, or stop working to improve things. You'll see this when we reach the section on 'taking a stand'. All I am saying is that *not good enough* is one of the mind's favourite stories, and when it hooks us and reels us in, our life usually gets harder.

Your mind may now come up with something like: *'How am I supposed to improve something if I don't first judge it as not good enough?'* Naturally, we will all encounter many things that we wish to improve in our lives. When this happens, we can acknowledge that there's a reality gap: a gap between what we want and what we've got. And after we've acknowledged it, we can get pro-active; we can figure out how to improve the situation and take effective action. This is very different to dwelling on the *not good enough* story: to replaying it all day long and stumbling around in a haze of discontentment. No matter how bad the situation, spending our days in a thick smog of *not good enough* will only make it worse than it already is.

When the *not good enough* story hooks us in, it's as if we pull on a pair of shit-coloured goggles. And when we peer at our marriage, or our body, or our job through these goggles, then guess what it looks like? And these goggles are pretty special: they don't just see things in the present, they can also see into the past and the future.

When we look through these goggles into the past, we replay old hurts and disappointments, we relive old losses and grievances, we reignite old resentments and ancient grudges, and we stew over painful events that can never be undone. Basically, our mind tells us that the past was *not good enough*.

Similarly, when we look at the future through those goggles, it isn't appealing. We see all sorts of scary scenarios, things that might and could go horribly wrong. We get bogged down in fears, worries and anxieties: fear of failure, fear of rejection, fear of getting old or sick, fear of screwing up our kids, fear of loneliness or poverty or injury, or fear of the uncertain and the unknown. In other words, the future is *not good enough*.

This story also underlies envy and greed: 'What I currently have is not good enough.' It underpins insecurity and a fear of intimacy: 'If you get to know me, you'll find out that I'm not good enough.' It feeds on resentment and anger: 'The way you're treating me is not good enough.' And it paves the way to depression and suicide: 'Life itself is not good enough.'

So what can we do about this story? Will positive thinking make it go away, counting our blessings and looking at the glass as half full? I doubt it. (You're welcome to try if you want, but millions have tried and failed.) What about if we get tough and tell ourselves firmly to stop being so judgemental, to stop thinking so negatively? Lots of people try this, but the irony is that it's just another way of judging yourself as *not good enough*. Luckily for us, there is a far more effective way of dealing with this story: notice it and name it.

When your mind is laying a trip on you about not achieving enough, or not earning enough, or not exercising enough, or accusing you of being fat, lazy, stupid, selfish, dumb, moody, anxious, pushy or wishy-washy, then the first step is simply to . . .

Pause.

Pause and breathe: a slow, deep, gentle inhalation.

Pause and breathe and notice. Notice what your mind is doing.

And as you notice your mind in action, be curious. Notice how your mind is telling you this story? Is it using words or pictures or a combination? Can you hear a voice inside your head? If so, where is it located: at the back of your head, or somewhere in the middle, or right at the top? And what does it sound like? Is it your voice or someone else's? Is it loud or soft or slow or fast? What is the emotion in the voice?

Then pause, breathe, notice and name.

Name the story in a way that helps you to separate, to step back and see it for what it is: a chain of words and pictures. For example, you might say to yourself, 'Aha! Here it is again. The old "*I'm* Not Smart Enough" story. I know this one!' And in that moment, you will probably notice a sense of lightness, as if you have just taken off those shit-coloured goggles and are now seeing the world with greater clarity.

This simple exercise is very empowering because it reminds us where our true power lies: not in trying to stop these stories from arising — not in doing battle with them — but in stepping back, seeing them for what they are, and letting them come and go in their own good time.

Suppose your mind is busy pointing out all the flaws, failings, annoying habits and weaknesses of your partner, children, friends, relatives or boss. If so, you can use the very same strategy: pause, breathe and notice. Notice your mind in action; notice how skilful it is at drawing you in. Be curious about the words that it chooses and the pictures it selects; notice how it splices them together to upset or anger or worry you. Pause, breathe, notice . . . then name the story: 'Aha! Here it is again. The "*He is/She is/They are* Not Good Enough" story.'

And if your mind is mouthing off about something non-human — your job, income, house, car or evening meal then pause, breathe, notice and name: 'Aha! The "*It's* Not Good Enough" story.'

Feel free to play around with this technique and bring some lightness and humour to it. For instance, you might playfully say to yourself, 'Tut, tut, tut! It's just noooooooooot good enough!' or 'Yippee! The Not Good Enough Show just started'. Or you might even name it with an abbreviation: 'NGE!'

See if you can tap into your natural warmth and humour as you notice and name your mind doing its stuff. See if you can appreciate the great irony that this wonderful instrument we call 'the human mind', which is so creative and innovative and immensely useful to us, came with an inbuilt tendency to judge, compare and criticise; to find fault, to focus on deficiencies, to see problems everywhere it looks.

If you're wondering why the human mind has this tendency, consider it in terms of evolution. The cavemen/women who lived long enough to have lots of children were those who could clearly see the current problems (e.g. dangerous animals, brutal weather and vicious rivals); those who could best anticipate future problems (e.g. *more* dangerous animals, brutal weather and vicious rivals); and those who could figure out how to solve these problems effectively. So if there ever was a caveman/woman who wandered around in a perpetual state of bliss, thinking that everything was good enough as it was, seeing no problems and anticipating no problems, then he or she wouldn't have survived long enough to have children. Way before they reached puberty, they would have been wiped out by the dangerous animals, brutal weather or vicious rivals.

Thus, as a result of evolution, our mind has evolved to be a super-duper problem-solving machine. And everywhere it looks it sees problems: things that are *not good enough* the way they are. (So if anyone has ever told you that 'negative thinking' is a sign of a defective or weak mind, clearly they don't know what they're talking about; it's a perfectly natural psychological process of a normal healthy human mind.)

Once we have noticed and named the *not good enough* story, we are generally able to separate from it, to put it down instead of holding on to it; to take off the goggles and look at the world with new eyes. Recall that mindfulness means paying attention with openness and curiosity. With the goggles off, we can bring our attention to what we see, hear, touch, taste and smell. We can notice, with curiosity, what we are doing here and now and we can fully engage in it, instead of wallowing in all that *NGE*.

Notice, we're not moving into the land of 'positive thinking' and trying to replace *NGE* with *EW* (*everything's wonderful*). That would be like trying to convince ourselves that the glass is half full instead of half empty. 'Half full' and 'half empty' are nothing more than stories about the glass, and neither is 'truer' than the other. When we are truly present with the glass, paying attention with openness and curiosity, those judgements about 'half full' or 'half empty' fade into the background; what comes into the foreground is the shape of the glass, the way it reflects the light, the level of the water within it, and the change in luminosity where the water touches its sides.

'Yes,' your mind might be saying, 'I can see that stewing on *not good enough* isn't helpful, but what do I do about the reality gap?' That's a great question. Whenever we face a reality gap, whether it be our marriage, job, health or behaviour, we can deal with it far more efficiently from a mental space of presence. It's hard to address problems effectively if we're lost in the smog.

However, getting present is only step one. Step two is clarifying your purpose: what do you want to stand for and how do you want to behave as you try to solve this problem? We'll cover step two later in the book when we look at the role of purpose but, for now, let's just stick with step one. Try unhooking yourself from *NGE* in whichever areas of life it shows up most often, and see what difference it makes. And once unhooked, bring a curious gaze to the world around you; 'be like a tree' and get present. And who knows? You may well find that when you lift up those murky goggles, your problems seem a little smaller or easier to live with.

Chapter II

THE WISDOM OF KINDNESS

At times the reality gap is forced upon us through disasters such as flood, famine, fire, death and disease. At other times we create the gap ourselves, at least in part, through our own self-defeating behaviour. We all screw up, get it wrong and make foolish mistakes. We all, at times, get jerked around by our emotions like a puppet on a string, and act in self-defeating ways. Entangled in our thoughts and struggling with our feelings, we end up saying and doing things that are far removed from the person we really want to be. We may hurt the people we love the most, or we may avoid them because we feel we are unworthy of their love.

As we practise and apply the principles within this book, we'll find this sort of thing happens less often but, the fact is, we will never be perfect. We will screw up again and again and again. This is part of being human.

So what does your mind tend to do when you screw up? If it's anything like my mind, it pulls out a big stick and starts whacking you; it tells you you're *not good enough*, or you can't do it, or there's something wrong with you; or it lectures you about the need to try harder, to do better and improve yourself. And this is hardly surprising. When we were growing up, adults often criticised us in an attempt to get us to change our behaviour; no wonder then that we grow up doing this to ourselves. Unfortunately, it isn't very helpful.

You've probably heard the old saying about 'the carrot and the stick'. If you want to get a donkey to carry your load, you can motivate it with a carrot or a stick. Both approaches will get the donkey moving but, over time, the more you hit that donkey with the stick, the more miserable and unhealthy it becomes. On the other hand, if you reward the donkey with a carrot whenever it does what you want, then over time, you end up with a much healthier donkey (with really good night vision!). Beating yourself up, coming down hard on yourself or getting stuck into yourself is just as ineffective as hitting a donkey with the stick. Sure, harsh self-criticism may sometimes get you moving in the right direction, but the more habitual it becomes, the more miserable and unhealthy you will be. It's highly unlikely to help you change your behaviour; it's far more likely to keep you feeling stuck and miserable.

So whatever created our reality gap, whether life cruelly dumped it on our doorstep or we made it (at least in part) through our own behaviour, to practise self-compassion is essential. (Unless, of course, you want to go through life like a battered donkey — but somehow I doubt that.)

Now you may recall that self-compassion has two elements: kindness and presence. We've already looked at the skills involved in presence: defusion, expansion and connection. The next step is to 'blend them' together with kindness. So I'm going to take you through an exercise (actually, more like a series of exercises) to give you the full experience of self-compassion.

An Exercise In Self-compassion

Find a comfortable position in which you are centred and alert. For example, if you're seated in a chair, you could lean slightly forwards, straighten your back, drop your shoulders and press your feet gently on to the floor.

Now bring to mind a reality gap you are struggling with. Take a few moments to reflect on the nature of this gap and how it is affecting you, and let your difficult thoughts and feelings arise.

1. BE PRESENT

Pause.

That's all you need do: just pause.

Pause for a few seconds and notice what your mind is telling you. Notice its choice of words, and the speed and volume of its speech.

Be curious: is this story old and familiar, or is it something new? What time zones is your mind taking you into: the past, present or future? What judgements is it making? What labels is it using?

Don't try to debate with your mind or try to silence it; you'll only stir it up.

Simply notice the story it's telling you.

And notice, with curiosity, all the different emotions that arise. What do you discover? Guilt, sadness, anger, fear or embarrassment? Resentment, despair, anguish, rage or anxiety?

Name these emotions as they arise: 'Here's fear' or 'Here's sadness'.

Pay attention, like a curious child, to what is going on inside your body. Where are you feeling these emotions the most? What are the size, shape and temperature of these feelings? How many layers do they have? How many different types of sensation can you find within them?

2. OPEN UP

Now slowly and deeply breathe into the pain.

Do so with an attitude of kindness.

Infuse this breath with caring and contribution; see it as an act of comfort and support.

Imagine your breath flowing into and around your pain.

Imagine that in some magical way, a vast space opens up inside you, making plenty of room for all those feelings.

No matter how painful they are, do not fight with them.

Offer peace to your feelings, rather than hostility.

Let them be as they are and give them plenty of space, rather than push them away.

And if you notice any resistance in your body — tightening, contraction or tension — breathe into that too. Make room for it.

Contribute peace and space to all that arises: your thoughts, your feelings and your resistance.

3. HOLD KINDLY

Now choose one of your hands.

Imagine this is the hand of someone very kind and caring.

Place this hand, slowly and gently, on whichever part of your body hurts the most.

Perhaps you feel the pain more in your chest, or perhaps in your head, neck or stomach? Wherever it is most intense, lay your hand there. (And if you've gone numb, or you can't locate any particular place, then simply rest your hand on the centre of your chest.)

Let it rest there, lightly and gently, either on your skin or your clothes.

Feel the warmth flowing from your palm to your body.

Imagine your body softening around the pain, loosening up, softening up and making space.

Hold this pain gently. Hold it as if it is a crying baby, or a whimpering puppy, or a fragile work of art.

Infuse this gentle action with caring and warmth, as if you are reaching out to someone you care about.

Let the kindness flow from your fingers.

Now, use both of your hands. Place one of them upon your chest and the other upon your stomach, and let them gently rest there. Hold yourself kindly and gently: connecting with yourself, caring for yourself, and contributing comfort and support.

4. SPEAK KINDLY

Now say something caring to yourself, to express concern or affection.

You might silently say a word like 'gentle' or 'kindness', to remind yourself of your intention.

You might say, 'This really hurts' or 'This is hard.'
You might say, 'I know this hurts, but I can do this.'
You might even repeat a quote, proverb or saying,
  as long as it does not make light of your pain.
If you've failed or made a mistake, then you might
  like to remind yourself, 'Yes, I'm human. Like
  everybody else on the planet, I fail and I make
  mistakes.'
You might acknowledge that this is part of being
  human; remind yourself, kindly and gently, this is
  what all humans feel when they face a reality gap.
  This pain tells you something very important: that
  you're alive, that you have a heart, that you care,
  and there's a gap between what you want and
  what you've got. And this is what all humans feel
  under such circumstances. It's unpleasant. It hurts.
  And you don't want it. And this is something you
  have in common with every other human being on
  the planet.

* * *

I hope you found the preceding exercise helpful. Obviously, modify the exercise as you wish. For example, if you don't like my suggestions for caring words, substitute your own. To help you with this, imagine yourself as a young child who is feeling the same pain as you. If you wanted to be kind to this child, to provide support or comfort, and to show that you truly care, then what kind words might you say? Whatever words spring to mind, try saying something similar to yourself, with that same attitude of care and concern and kindness. You can even go a step further with this idea and turn it into a powerful imaginary exercise, as follows:

Compassion For The Younger You

Find a comfortable position and close your eyes or stare at a spot.

Take a few slow, deep breaths and notice them with openness and curiosity.

You are about to do an exercise in imagination. Some people imagine with vivid, colourful pictures, much like those on a TV screen; others imagine with vague, fuzzy, unclear pictures; while others imagine without using pictures at all, relying more on words and ideas. However you imagine is just fine.

Now imagine yourself getting into a time machine. Once inside that machine, you travel back in time to visit yourself as a young child. Visit this child at some point in their life when they are in a lot of pain, immediately after some distressing childhood event.

Now step out of the time machine and make contact with the younger you. Take a good look at this young child and get a sense of what he is going through. Is she crying? Is he angry or frightened? Does she feel guilty or ashamed? What does this child really need: love, kindness, understanding, forgiveness, nurturing or acceptance? In a kind, calm and gentle voice, tell this 'younger you' that you know what just happened, that you know what he's been through; that you know how much she is hurting.

Tell this child that he doesn't need anyone else to

validate that experience because YOU know.

Tell this child that she survived the experience and it is now just a painful memory.

Tell this child that you are here, that you know how much it hurts and you want to help in any way you can.

Ask this child if there's anything she needs or wants from you — and whatever she asks for, give it to her. If this child asks you to take him somewhere special, go ahead and do it. Offer a hug, a kiss, words of kindness, or a gift of some sort. This is an exercise in imagination, so you can give anything she wants. If this younger you doesn't know what he wants, or doesn't trust you, then let him know that's fine; that you are here for support, and will always be there to do whatever you can to help.

Tell this child that you are here, that you care, and that you are going to help her recover from this pain to go on to lead a full, rich and valued life.

Continue to radiate caring and kindness towards this younger you, in any way you can think of through words, gestures or deeds.

Once you have a sense that this younger you has accepted your caring and kindness, let her be and bring awareness to your breathing.

Observe your breathing with openness and curiosity for a couple of minutes, then open your eyes and connect with the room around you.

* * *

Many people find that it is much easier to be compassionate

towards a young child in pain than it is to be compassionate towards themselves — the exercise above makes good use of that fact. It's good to practise it on a regular basis, not only for developing self-compassion, but also for healing old wounds.

Aside from practising these exercises, think about the actions you could take: small acts of kindness you can do for yourself. How about a soothing hot bath or shower? Getting a massage? Eating some nutritious, healthy food? Going for a walk? Giving yourself some 'me time'? Listening to your favourite music?

Can you listen to yourself non-judgementally and acknowledge the extent of your pain? Can you treat yourself gently and give yourself the benefit of the doubt? Can you recognise you're a fallible human being so of course you make mistakes? Can you look for the goodness in yourself? (It is definitely in there, no matter how much your mind may deny it.)

I know this is easier said than done but, like every new skill, self-compassion takes practice. Personally, I find it hardest when I have yelled at my son. At times I get very cross with him and lose my temper. Why? Because he is not behaving the way my mind wants him to; he is not learning or developing at the rate my mind says he *should* be. Fused with these stories, I lose touch with my values of patience and acceptance and then I snap or yell or say harsh words.

Then moments later, my mind comes out with the big stick: 'Bad father!', 'What a lousy job you're doing!', 'What a hypocrite you are!', 'He's just a five-year-old kid; go easy on him; what are you losing your temper for?', 'Call yourself an ACT therapist?', 'What would the readers of your books think if they could see you now?'

And before I know it, I am flailing around in a huge emotional storm of guilt, anger, embarrassment or frustration.

And then . . . after a while . . . I realise what is going on and I plant my feet on the floor and I take some deep breaths and I notice what I can see, hear, touch, taste and smell. I connect with the world; I get present. And I acknowledge that I am hurting. And then I gently place a hand on my chest or my abdomen — wherever it hurts the most — and I breathe deeply. And I remind myself: 'You're a human being. And like every other parent on the planet, you screw up sometimes. This is what it feels like when you really care about being a good parent and you don't manage to live up to your own ideals.'

And then I look deeper at what's underneath all that anger and frustration and what I find down there is ENORMOUS FEAR — so much fear about my son's future: about what will happen to him if he doesn't 'progress' enough. Will he be rejected or picked on? Will he be that kid in the class that everyone teases or makes jokes about?

And then I look deeper still, to see what is beneath all that fear. And there it is: LOVE. Nothing but sheer, boundless, magical, never-ending love.

And if you make the time to sit quietly, to be kind and gentle with yourself, and take a curious look at your emotional pain, then I suspect you will find something similar inside yourself. Whatever the emotion is — anger, fear, sadness or guilt — hold it gently and ask yourself: 'What does this pain reveal about my heart? What does it show me that I care about?' Or ask yourself this question, which comes from Steve Hayes, the originator of ACT: 'What would you have to not care about, in order to not have this pain?'

These questions help you to remember that you are not 'bad', even if your mind says you are. You are a caring human being. After all, if you didn't care, you wouldn't hurt.

Think Small

To develop self-compassion, we don't have to do something big and dramatic. The tiniest act of kindness makes a difference. For example, here are a few acts I have done this morning: I stretched my back and neck, I had a hot shower, I played with the cats, I tickled and wrestled with my son, I ate a healthy breakfast, and I listened to the birds outside the window. Such tiny acts of caring and contribution build up over time into a supportive, compassionate relationship with yourself. And even if you just *imagine* doing these acts, then, that in itself, can generate a sense of self-kindness.

US psychologist Kristin Neff, one of the world's top researchers on self-compassion, recommends a third key element in addition to mindfulness and kindness, which we touched on in the exercise above: she calls it 'commonality' or 'common humanity'. Basically this involves reflecting on the human condition and the nature of suffering. When we are hurting and suffering, let's remind ourselves that these are *normal* human experiences; that all over the planet, in this moment, there are millions upon millions of other human beings suffering in ways very similar to our own. We don't do this to discount or trivialise our pain, but rather to acknowledge it as part of being human; as something we have in common with everyone else; as something that can help us to understand the suffering of others and extend our compassion to them too.

Often when we're suffering, our mind tells us that we are the only one. That everybody else out there is happier than we are! That others don't feel the pain that we feel. That others don't screw up or make mistakes or fail — at least, not to the same extent that we do. And if we buy this story, it will make our suffering all the more intense. The reality is, all humans suffer. Every human life will be touched by loss and hardship. We all feel the slap and face the gap; it happens over and over, for every human being on the planet.

So when life knocks us around, or dumps a pile of manure

on our doorstep, remember: self-compassion comes first. Once that's in place, it's often useful to turn to strategising and problem solving; reflecting on words of wisdom and taking committed action guided by our values. But the best results will usually occur when compassion comes first.

So, please don't wait another moment. I encourage you to build self-compassion at every opportunity; it is the key to true inner strength. Throughout your day, practise tiny acts of self-kindness. Each and every one of them makes a difference.

PART 3

DROP THE ANCHOR

Chapter 12

ANCHORS AWAY

Clearly, there is no escaping the fact that the bigger the reality gap, the greater our emotional pain. And there are two emotions in particular that will almost always show up in these difficult times: fear and anger. This is hardly surprising. When any fish, reptile, bird or mammal experiences a significant threat, its 'fight-or-flight' response is triggered: the organism gets ready to either run away from the threat, or to stay and fight it off. In humans, the 'fight' response instantly turns into anger (or its close relatives: frustration, irritation, resentment and rage). Likewise, the 'flight' response instantly turns into fear (or its close relatives: anxiety, 'nerves', doubt, insecurity and panic). And very commonly, we experience both the 'fight' and 'flight' emotions at the same time.

On top of anger and fear, there may be all sorts of other painful emotions. For example, if the gap involves a significant loss of some sort, sadness and sorrow will arise. And if we have somehow contributed to this gap (or at least, if we believe we have) then guilt is also highly likely to show up.

These painful feelings are often like a tidal wave: they rise up and bowl us over and carry us away, often before we are even aware of it. And, you may be surprised to hear this, but there's a time and a place to allow this to happen: to let ourselves be engulfed by the waves. Why? Because no matter how big they are, those waves can't drown us (even though the mind will claim that they will). You see, when we access a mental state of expansion — when we 'step back' and look at those waves with openness and curiosity — we become like the sky: vast, open and spacious. And no matter how turbulent our emotions are, we can make room for them and let them come and go, just as waves rise up from the ocean and then fall back in.

When we're in great pain, it's helpful to keep ourselves anchored, but obviously there will be times when we'll fail to do this. Still, as soon as we realise we've been swept away, we can, instantaneously, drop the anchor. And over time, it will get easier. The waves will gradually start to reduce in size. They may still be large, but they're no longer tidal waves. And sometimes they'll knock us over, but sometimes they won't. And the better and faster we get at dropping the anchor, the less impact those waves will have when they hit us.

How then do we go about dropping the anchor? Well, as it happens, you already know: it's just an ultra-brief version of 'Be Like A Tree', which we aim to do in the space of five to ten seconds. How about we run through it right now?

Drop The Anchor

Take five to ten seconds to do the following:

Push your feet hard on to the floor and straighten
 your spine.
As you do this, take a slow deep breath.
Look around and notice five things you can see.
Listen carefully and notice five things you can hear.
Notice where you are and what you are doing.

---

* * *

This very brief exercise can be done at any time and in any place, and it instantly brings us back into the present so we can engage in life and focus on the task at hand. And if we maintain an expansive awareness of our surroundings, our actions and our feelings, this will usually keep us anchored until the wave subsides.

As with any mindfulness exercise, there are all sorts of ways that you can modify it. For instance, you could stand up and give your body a stretch, and hold that stretch, and feel your muscles lengthen. Or you could push your palms hard against each other and feel the muscles contract in your neck, arms and shoulders. Or you could press your hands down hard on the arms of your chair. Or firmly massage the back of your neck and scalp.

Then, using these physical sensations as your anchor, open your ears and reach out to the world. Notice what you can see, hear, touch, taste and smell; notice where you are and what you are doing. And you can do all this as quickly or as slowly as you like.

In practice, 'dropping anchor' and 'holding yourself kindly' happen almost simultaneously. Sometimes we may drop anchor first and then rapidly follow up with a bit of self-compassion, and sometimes it may be the other way around.

Remember Ali, the Iraqi refugee who had been tortured? I asked him to practise dropping anchor at least twenty to thirty times a day. That may seem like a lot, but he was suffering from PTSD (Post-traumatic stress disorder) and I knew it would take him a long time to recover. I knew those flashbacks would continue to hijack him, to pounce on him unexpectedly and carry him off to the past to relive his nightmares. So I wanted him to become an expert at returning to the present. And I strongly encourage you to do the same.

Of course, it's not just painful emotions that sweep us away;

we also get easily carried off by our thoughts, especially by that old 'not good enough' story, which rarely goes for long without dropping in on us. The *NGE* story is very crafty. It continually changes its appearance with different disguises, which makes it all the harder for us to spot it, and allows it to easily catch us unawares. So to get better at spotting these different disguises, let's look at this story's role in some common reality gaps.

Envy and Jealousy

Sam, a wealthy entrepreneur, was frequently affected by envy. Even though he was a multimillionaire, he did not see himself as wealthy. Why? Because he compared himself to all the entrepreneurs he knew who were *billionaires*. And whenever he heard of their successes, he was almost sick; his stomach would churn, his jaw would clamp tight and his heart would pound away like a wild beast. Then bitter and resentful, he'd wonder why they had the wealth and not him.

We all at times get caught up in envy or jealousy. These unpleasant emotions occur when we see the good fortune of others, but rather than rejoice in it, we resent it; we want what they have for ourselves. Our minds are so quick to compare and judge, it happens before we realise it. We see (or hear about, or fantasise about) that other person's career, partner, car, house, income, looks, intelligence or personality — and our mind compares it with our own and judges ours as *not good enough*. We then feel a sense of deprivation, unfairness or missing out.

In other words, we get hooked by *NGE*. Our minds tell us: 'What I already have is *not good enough*. I need more, or better quality, or both. I need to have what they have!' In Sam's case, his mind said his income was 'not *large* enough', his business was 'not *successful* enough', and he had 'not *achieved* enough'. What does your mind say to you to stir up envy? Does it focus on certain aspects of your life? Are there certain key topics where it knows it can easily grab you?

Personally, my mind likes to taunt me about my book sales. I remember a particular incident a couple of years back. I was chatting to Steven Hayes about his self-help book *Get Out of Your Mind and Into Your Life,* and when he told me how many copies he had sold, I was absolutely flooded with envy. His sales figures were way more than mine. I tried hard to smile as I congratulated him, but I suspect I looked pale and stricken, and inside I felt as if I'd been kicked in the guts.

Obviously my reaction was not rational. If you read the acknowledgements page in any of my self-help books, you'll always find Steve's name near the top; I am incredibly grateful to this man and the rational reaction would have been to rejoice in his success. Indeed, once I had calmed down and applied the advice in this book, I *was* able to appreciate his good fortune. However, my initial reaction was envy and it came on so fast and so strong, it really shocked me. After all, my own book, *The Happiness Trap,* was also doing very well, and prior to this encounter with Steve, I had been more than satisfied with its sales. It just goes to show the power of the mind; how in one split second it can strip away any sense of fulfilment and replace it with major dissatisfaction.

Now let's not forget there's also the possessive form of jealousy: the jealous husband or wife who gets anxious, angry or paranoid when their partner spends time (or wishes to do so) with others. In this case, the jealous partner usually has two versions of *NGE*. First, there's often a deep-seated '*I'm* not good enough, and if my partner spends time with others, she will find out that they're better than me.' This is commonly linked to a second *NGE*: 'My partner is *not* loyal/trustworthy/faithful/honest *enough*, so eventually she will leave or deceive me.'

At the core of jealousy and envy, we tend to find fear. It may take many different forms: fear of material loss or poverty; fear of underachieving, or of being found wanting, or of being rejected for not measuring up; fear of missing out or 'settling for less'. And as you can see, all these different fears are thematically linked to the idea of *not good enough*. So when we're struggling with envy or jealousy or possessiveness, the first step is to identify the *NGE* story. Ask yourself: 'What is my mind telling me is *not good enough*? Is it my body, my mind, my life, my achievements, my job, my income, my kids or my partner?'

The next steps are to name it, let go and drop anchor; then engage in whatever you are doing and act with purpose. However, keep in mind that while defusion from *NGE* is certainly helpful, it's only one part of the picture. We also need to deal with the physical reaction: to make room for those unpleasant feelings and practise self-compassion.

Self-compassion is especially important. Envy and jealousy, along with the fears at their core, and the resentments layered on top of them, are painful and difficult experiences. These emotions hurt, and when we get caught up in them, we suffer. So let's be kind and caring to ourselves.

And be wary: our minds may use our own reactions as ammunition against us; they may judge us harshly for having such reactions in the first place. For example, when I reflected on my envy towards Steven Hayes, I did not like what it revealed: it highlighted my insecurities and my sense of inadequacy. Was my mind compassionate and understanding about this? Did it say to me, 'Russ, you're a human being and such emotional reactions are perfectly normal and common-place, so go easy on yourself'? No, it did not — at least, not initially. Instead, my mind pulled out a big stick, gave me a massive hiding, and called me all sorts of rude names. We need to be on the lookout for such reactions: self-judgement, self-recrimination, self-punishment and self-blame. They do nothing, absolutely nothing, to help us. They are all simply versions of 'I'm not good enough', so we need to notice them, name them and let go, and practise being kind to ourselves instead.

Sam, the entrepreneur, was initially very sceptical about this approach, but I encouraged him to try it and, gradually, his envy and harsh self-judgement began to diminish. He had always achieved results through being hard on himself, so being self-compassionate did not come naturally. However, over time, he built a beautiful relationship with himself, and as he did so, comparing himself to his peers became much less important.

Loneliness

Loneliness is another very common reality gap. However, it's important to recognise that loneliness is not the same as 'being alone'. You have probably had the experience (at least occasionally) of being alone and actually enjoying your solitude. Loneliness is, at its core, a state of disconnection: a turning away from reality, rather than engaging with it. And this disconnection can happen even while we're in the midst of social interaction; thus the common saying: 'I was so lonely in that relationship.' It can also exhibit itself as the unpleasant sense of disconnection we all experience when someone is with us physically, but they're 'not really present'.

In this state of disconnection, unpleasant thoughts and feelings arise and we tend to call this experience 'loneliness'. The thoughts convey the idea that our reality here and now is *not good enough*: 'I wish someone else was here', or 'I wish I was somewhere else'. As for the feelings, they are usually a mixture of sadness, longing and anxiety, sometimes mixed with frustration or resentment.

When we look at loneliness this way, we can see that defusing from our thoughts and making room for our feelings is part of the answer, but not the whole of it. Our loneliness is both a signal that we're disconnected and a reminder that we value connection. After all, if we didn't value connection, we wouldn't feel lonely, right? So the other part of the answer is to actively cultivate connection.

Now we could cultivate connection with other people, but that might not be possible, or we may choose not to. So if we can't or won't cultivate that connection with others, we can cultivate it with ourselves, through self-compassion. We can also create that connection with nature, our work, our hobbies, our sport, our religion, our art, or anything else that meets these two conditions:

a) it is available to us in this moment, and

b) it matters to us in some way.

To connect with these things, we take action: we start doing some form of activity that plays a role in this domain of our life. We give that activity our full attention and step out of our thoughts and engage 100 per cent in what we are doing.

Often as we do this, we become so absorbed in the activity that those lonely thoughts and feelings disappear. However, when this happens, it's a bonus; not the main aim. Our aim is to lead a life based on presence and purpose, not to try to get rid of unpleasant feelings. So if those thoughts and feelings *don't* disappear, it's really not a problem; provided we respond with expansion and defusion, they can't stop us from having a life-enhancing connection with something important.

Diagnostic Labels

Many therapists, psychologists and psychiatrists place great importance on giving their clients a diagnosis: labelling them with a mental disorder, such as major depressive disorder, generalised anxiety disorder, panic disorder, obsessive-compulsive disorder, post-traumatic stress disorder, or literally hundreds of others. And while this diagnosis is undoubtedly of help in some contexts, it can also be very harmful in others. *If* this diagnosis helps us to make positive life changes, then in that context we could say that it's helpful.

But if we fuse with this diagnostic label — if we believe that this label is who we are, that it sums us up and that it captures our essence, then we're in trouble. And, sadly, this is quite a common occurrence. I've met many clients who got stuck in life when they fused with their own labels: 'I am a depressive', 'I am obsessive-compulsive', or 'I am an addict'. Notice the effect of describing yourself in this way: it makes it sound like you *are* the label; as if this diagnosis is *you*.

And to make matters worse, these labels commonly attach to many other versions of *not good enough*: 'I'm damaged goods', 'I don't think rationally', 'There is something wrong with me', 'I can't cope as well as other people', 'I'm weak', 'I'm different', or 'I'm screwed up'.

Now at this point a reminder: in ACT we generally don't look at these stories in terms of true or false; what we're interested in is whether or not they are helpful. In other words, if I hold on tightly to this story, will it help me to be the person I want to be, or do the things that make my life richer and fuller? Sadly, at least in my experience, many people who fuse with these diagnostic labels find it *doesn't* help them live richer lives. It holds them back because they fuse with a belief such as: 'I can't do [insert important goal] because I am [insert diagnostic label].' And when they hold on tightly to this belief and allow it to push them around and dictate what they do, then it usually becomes a self-fulfilling prophecy.

So the message is, hold these labels lightly. The label of ingredients on a jam jar is not the same thing as the jam itself. And the description of a resort in a travel brochure is not the same thing as the resort itself. Likewise, any diagnostic label is simply a description of thoughts, feelings and behaviours: it is not the same thing as the person who has these thoughts, feelings and behaviours.

And that message applies equally to labels on others. For when other people get labelled in this manner, we can easily start to see them through the lens of their diagnosis. And that is not healthy for a relationship: it's looking at the other person as being *not good enough*. My wife and I both fell into this trap when our son was first diagnosed with autism. We both instantly fused with that label and the effect on us was horrendous. We felt as if our son had been taken from us; as if our little boy had disappeared and in his place was this huge, oppressive diagnosis.

Luckily, over time, we defused from the label. We learned to hold it very lightly; to see it as merely a tool to help us access services that could make a difference. Our little boy came back again; we could appreciate him and enjoy his eccentricities. We could accept his challenges and relish our many wonderful times together, rather than seeing him as a case of Autism Spectrum Disorder.

And obviously this approach is relevant to all forms of NGE labels, not just psychiatric diagnoses. If we are fused with labels such as 'fat', 'stupid', 'loser', 'worthless', 'ugly', 'lazy', 'incompetent', 'inadequate' and so on — whether they apply to others or ourselves — let's recognise that it's unhelpful and unhook ourselves.

Can You Spot the NGE?

If you want more insight into the prevalence of the *NGE* story, you may wish to consider its role in resentment, greed, perfectionism, boredom, insecurity or shame. Explore any of these experiences and you'll always find the same two major elements: unpleasant sensations in your body and a storyline [*] based on *NGE*. And either one of these elements, or more commonly both of them together, can sweep us away in a moment. So it pays to get good at dropping anchor. *grounding*

Reality gaps vary enormously in size: some are huge — leading to shock, grief, despair or rage; others are small — leading to disappointment, frustration or irritation; and others are somewhere in-between. However, no matter how great or small these gaps may be, we always have a choice in how we react with them. If a reality gap *can* be closed (without opening another one that's even bigger), then it makes sense that we take action to close it. But if it *can't* be closed, at least not for the time being, then instead of running or fighting, we can simply drop anchor: unhook from our unhelpful stories, make room for our painful emotions, and engage fully in doing something with purpose.

[handwritten note]

* The storyline of NGE is based on underline program of WANTING APPROVAL/DIS-approval — (control issue. giving rise 2 control strategies
NGE = PERFECTIONISM

Chapter 13

COMING HOME 2 My BODY in the HERE Now

I'm sitting here in front of my computer, trying hard to engage in what I am doing. My mind is telling me all sorts of unhelpful stories. None of them are new. I know all of them intimately. They come to visit almost every time I write. Loudest today is the 'fraud' story. This one points out that if my readers knew me well — if they could see all the times I get lost in my own psychological smog, or allow my feelings to push me around, or run from my painful emotions instead of making room for them — they'd be horrified. They'd see me as a fraud, a fake and an impostor and denounce me as the world's biggest hypocrite.

Almost as loud is the 'boring' story. This one tells me I have nothing new to say, that I'm just regurgitating the same old stuff and my readers will be bored out of their minds. It is accompanied in its chorus by the 'impending deadline' story. This one tells me how many thousands of words I still have to write, and how little time I have left to do it.

Tagging along at the back is the 'too hard' story. This one is whispering seductively in my ear: 'Give up, give up, give up.' It's very quiet, but very persistent. 'It's all too hard,' it murmurs, 'you've run out of steam. You've got nothing new to say. Give up, give up, give up.' And then it tempts me. It speaks to me of fun, of pleasure, of movies, of food, of sleeping, of reading, of music; of all the things I could be doing that are so much more enjoyable than writing.

I notice the struggle arising within myself. Anxiety and frustration surface and I feel the urge to fight and resist these feelings.

Then my mind brings out the stick and starts whacking me: 'Why do I do this? Why do I bring this on myself? Why do I agree to these ridiculous deadlines?' And there's that whispering again: 'Give up, give up, give up. Why don't you give up writing and do something easier?'

I notice the urge to pull away, to quit and run.

I notice my desire to escape from this discomfort, to get rid of all this tension.

And it would be so easy to do so. All I need to do is get up from my computer, walk away and do something less challenging.

'Yes,' whispers the voice. 'Just walk away.'

The smog is thickening and, beneath it, hot emotions bubble away.

What should I do?

In the midst of this emotional storm, I drop an anchor.

I push my feet firmly on to the floor.

And I take a slow deep breath.

First I exhale, pushing all the air out of my lungs. Then I allow them to fill by themselves from the bottom upwards.

My chest expands. My belly rises.

I can feel myself opening up and expanding.

There is a sense of space and lightness in my chest: a sense of opening up around my heart.

I am coming home. I am coming back home to my body and getting in touch.

I feel my shoulder blades sliding gently downwards.

I tune into my heart. I feel it opening. There is warmth, tenderness and fear.

I breathe into it once more. There is a sense of opening, of flowering.

With childlike curiosity, I observe my mind. It is slowing down, speaking more softly, laying down the stick.

I breathe and expand, softening and opening.

I remember to be gentle with myself.

I scan my body for any remaining resistance. And I rapidly find it: two thick cords of tension, running down my neck and into my shoulders.

I breathe into the tension, making no attempt to get rid of it; aiming purely and simply to give it space and allow it to be. And as I do so, it releases.

And noticing that flow of breath, of warmth and of kindness, I bring my attention back to the task at hand. Is it meaningful, is it important?

Yes, it is. This work matters to me. It is deeply aligned with my purpose.

So, gently and patiently, I return my attention to the task.

I am coming back home to my life in the here and now; coming back home to the tasks that I choose to do.

And I ask myself: 'Can I let go of having to "do it right" or "get it finished"?'

This is meaningful work. I don't want to rush through it with a sense of obligation or resentment. Can I bring an attitude of openness and curiosity to it? Can I do it calmly and peacefully, from a place of caring and giving? Can I infuse it with simplicity and compassion?

Yes. I can.

So I sit up in the chair, straighten my back, place my fingers on the keyboard and I do what matters.

***

And that is what writing is like for me. Again and again, I get hijacked by my own thoughts and feelings. They catch me off guard and I forget to respond mindfully. Instead of presence, defusion and expansion, I get lost in the smog, or I clutch at control, or I allow myself to be controlled.

And then . . . I remember. And I get present.

And then I forget again.

And then I remember again.

And so on. This is the nature of presence.

Moments of presence are easy; sustaining it is difficult.

Our attention loves to wander; it is hard to keep it in one spot for very long. So we must practise catching it. Our attention drifts, we notice it has gone and we catch it and bring it back. We get lost in the smog, we notice we're lost and we get present. We get pulled into a struggle with our feelings, we notice we're entangled and we expand. And we do this again and again for the rest of our lives. We never reach some perfect state where it is no longer necessary to do this. No one is fully present all the time — not even Zen masters. It's the same for all of us: in some moments we are present; in others we are not.

Of course, some people are far more present than others and this is largely due to the amount of practice they do. Now so far in this book, I've only spoken about informal practice: quick and simple mindfulness exercises that you can do throughout the day. But if you'd like to really develop your capacity for presence, you may also want to consider a formal practice, such as mindfulness meditation or Hatha yoga or Tai Chi.

There's one particular formal practice that is incredibly useful and I highly recommend it: mindfulness of the breath. It involves focusing attention on your breathing and bringing it back repeatedly, no matter how often it wanders. In Appendix 2, you'll find a detailed description of the exercise. A word of warning, though: if you've never done an exercise like this before, you will be shocked at how challenging it is. If you can stay focused on your breath for even ten seconds before your attention wanders to something else, you'll be doing well.

One of the greatest challenges in self-development is perfectionism. We all know that there's no such thing as being perfect — we all have flaws, we all make mistakes, and there's always room for improvement. However, most of us have a tendency to forget this. Our minds are quick to tell us that we should be trying harder, we should be doing better, we shouldn't settle for anything less than the best. And before we know it, we are slaves. We bang the drum and toil away, sweating, tense and nervous, terrified we might not reach our full potential. We double-check and triple-check for mistakes, never quite trusting we have found them all. We repeatedly go back and start again, or we give up altogether because we'll never measure up to our own expectations. And we are merciless when we fail or 'underachieve'; we crack the whip and beat ourselves senseless.

Of course, perfectionism is just another version of the 'not good enough' story. As are all the personal stories I mentioned at the beginning of this chapter: 'fraud', 'boring', 'too hard' and 'deadline'. Clearly the 'not good enough' story takes thousands of different forms, but we deal with them all the same way: notice them and name them.

Trying to be perfect doesn't help. Mindfulness skills can never be perfected; they can only be improved and every moment of practice makes a difference. Even if we spend a whole week lost in the smog — or even a month or a year — the moment we catch ourselves, we are free. We are free to choose. We can choose to stay in the smog, or we can choose to do something far more fulfilling: to notice and name the story and get back to the present.

Now I have to admit, when it comes to applying this knowledge to myself, there is plenty of room for improvement.

I have good days and bad days, strong moments and weak ones. But over time, I have got better. These days I do much less running from the reality gap, less fighting and railing against it. Instead, I tend to come back to the present and look with curious eyes on my life in this moment. And I ask myself this question: 'What do I want to stand for in the face of this?' This is one of those big questions that we will all need to answer many times. And it leads us on to the next section of this book.

PART 4

TAKE A STAND

Chapter 14

WHAT'S MY PURPOSE?

In my mid-twenties, I often thought about killing myself. People who knew me at that time are always shocked to hear this. My friends, family and work colleagues had no idea how miserable I was because I was excellent at hiding it. I managed to convince everyone around me that I was happy, fulfilled and content.

And certainly, to the outside observer, there was no good reason for me to be miserable. If anything, I seemed to 'have it all'. I had emigrated from cold, rainy England to warm, sunny Australia. I had bought a lovely house in a funky neighbourhood in one of the world's most exciting cities (Melbourne). As a young doctor, I had a highly respected, well-paid and very stimulating job. I also had an unusual and very rewarding hobby: stand-up comedy. I regularly performed as 'Dr Russ' around the comedy clubs of Melbourne, which was not only a fantastic buzz, but also earned me money, praise and fame. (Not huge fame or money, by any stretch, but it was a good earner and I did get several appearances on prime-time Australian TV shows such as *Tonight Live* and *The Midday Show*.)

And yet, even with all this, I was deeply unhappy. There were several contributing factors, not least of which was a harsh 'inner critic': an ongoing stream of self-judgemental thoughts. But first and foremost was a pervasive sense of meaninglessness.

'What is it all about?' I often wondered. Sure, I had a good job, a good house, a good income, a good hobby, but so what? Was that it? Was that all there was to life? I had all sorts of ways of generating pleasure — buying clothes, books, CDs; going to the movies; eating out at top restaurants; drinking fine wine; taking up interesting hobbies such as scuba-diving; going on exotic holidays; and so on. But while it was all enjoyable, none of that fulfilled me. I had no sense of purpose. I was just going through my days, ticking the boxes and trying, without much luck, to feel happy. Surely there had to be more to life than this?

Eventually, my misery started me on a quest: a journey to find the answers, not just for myself, but for the many patients I saw who seemed to struggle with very similar issues to my own. And what I discovered was that in order to find the big answers, you first have to ask some big questions:

- What truly matters to me, deep in my heart?
- What do I want to stand for with my time on this planet?
- What sort of human being do I want to be?
- How do I want to behave towards myself, others and the world around me?
- What personal qualities do I want to cultivate?

Consider these 'big questions' for a while before reading on.

* * *

Presence and purpose are intimate partners. Purpose gives our life direction, and presence allows us to make the most of the journey. If you have presence without purpose, it's like being on a yacht without sails: you are adrift and at the mercy of the elements, with no control over your direction. Many people think that purpose can be found in something external — such as a relationship or a career. But the truth is, purpose is something you find within yourself.

I certainly found this to be true in my early years as a doctor. You might expect that a career in medicine comes pre-loaded with purpose: caring for others, healing the sick, compassion for those in pain. But it is not necessarily so. I am embarrassed to admit that as a junior doctor, I lacked compassion for my patients. I was disconnected from them and insensitive to their thoughts and feelings. I saw my job as basically to get them better and get them out of hospital as soon as possible, through efficiently providing the best medical treatment. So if they got sicker, or failed to recover quickly, instead of compassion, I felt annoyed; I saw them as a 'nuisance', making my job harder. The idea of forming a deep, compassionate connection with my patients never even popped into my head. On those rare occasions when I would catch sight of a colleague having a truly caring, heart-to-heart talk with a patient, I would shake my head and wonder in amazement: *who has time for that?!*

This disconnection and insensitivity towards my patients made my job very unsatisfying and it took me a long, long time to realise it. Funnily enough, what first opened my eyes was a Hollywood movie called *The Doctor* starring William Hurt. *The Doctor* is based on the true story of a heart surgeon who is technically brilliant at cardiac surgery, but lacks empathy and compassion for his patients. However, all that changes when he gets a taste of his own medicine. When he is diagnosed with throat cancer, he finds himself in the care of a doctor much like himself: technically brilliant, but cold and insensitive. And he doesn't like it. So he transfers to the care of another doctor who is kind, caring and compassionate. I don't want to tell you the whole story; I encourage you to watch the film. However, what I can tell you is that by the end of the movie this cardiac surgeon has discovered the incredible importance of compassion.

I first saw *The Doctor* in 1994, by which time I was working as a GP in private practice — and it was a 'light bulb moment'. I thought to myself, '*That's* how I want to be: compassionate, caring and sensitive.' And the very next day, I consciously started bringing those qualities into my work. I started to slow down my consultations and take the time to ask my patients about their feelings; to empathise with their pain and their fear; to infuse my speech and my gestures with genuine caring and kindness.

The results were amazing. Not only did my patients respond positively, but my work became far more satisfying and so much more *meaningful*.

However, there were other consequences that weren't quite so wonderful. You see, as I became more caring, my consultations grew longer. And longer. And even longer. In my early years as a GP, they had averaged eight minutes, but within a year of making this shift in my attitude, I was averaging thirty minutes per consultation. And during these sessions, we would spend at least half of the time talking about my patients' feelings, challenges, hopes, dreams and aspirations — rather than their medical conditions. All well and good, but what I hadn't foreseen was this: as my consultations grew longer, my income went down and down.

You see, back then in Australia, the Medicare system worked like this: GPs who saw a large number of patients for a brief time each, earned far more money than those who saw a small number of patients for a long time each. So by the time I was averaging thirty minutes per patient, my income had dropped by half! And yet, surprisingly, I didn't really mind. Why? Because I was far more fulfilled. My life was much richer and the trade-off was worth every cent. Indeed, I found this caring, compassionate connection with my patients so rewarding that I ultimately changed careers so I could have even more of it: I retrained as a psychotherapist. And guess what happened to my income? That's right, it dropped even further — to less than a third of what I had once earned as a GP.

But again, it was well worth the trade-off. As my income plummeted, my sense of fulfilment soared. And that is why I have never once regretted that decision. It took me on a long and winding path, which ultimately led to a much richer and fuller life (and to writing books such as this one), and it confirmed to me the old saying that money can't buy you happiness. (That old saying, by the way, has also been confirmed with lots of good scientific research.)

Finding Purpose

Every action we take serves a purpose. From doing the washing to eating an ice-cream; from getting married to filling in a tax return; from zoning out in front of late-night TV to going for an early morning jog: underlying each and every action, there is always some sort of intention — we are taking action to make something happen. But how often are we conscious of this intention? And how often do our actions *consciously* serve some greater purpose that personally matters to us?

For most of us, the answer to both questions is: 'not too often'. Our tendency is to go through life on autopilot, rather than consciously choosing what we do and how we go about doing it. The problem with this is that we may end up spending large chunks of our days acting in ways that are largely unfulfilling. However, if we consciously align our actions to a chosen purpose — to a cause that is personally important — then everything changes. Our life becomes imbued with meaning. We develop a sense of direction; of creating the life we want. And we experience a sense of vitality and fulfilment that is wholly missing from life on autopilot.

When I ask my clients about their purpose in life, the most common reactions I get are confusion, anxiety or 'I don't know'. (The few exceptions are clients who already have a strong sense of purpose either from their religion or from previous personal development.) So I ask them the 'big questions' as above, and this starts to get them thinking. In ACT we refer to this process as clarifying values, and it's a very important thing to do, because it's our values that infuse our life with purpose.

So what are values, exactly? They are your heart's deepest desires for how you want to behave as a human being; they are the qualities you want to bring to your ongoing actions. They are different to goals in that goals can be completed or achieved, ticked off the list and finished, whereas values are ongoing until the day you die.

If you're a little confused by this concept, you're not alone. We live in a goal-focused society, not a values-focused one. Indeed, often when people use the word 'values' they are really talking about rules or goals, so let me clarify the difference. Values are about *how you want to behave,* while goals are about *what you want to get*. If you want to get a great job, buy a big house, find a partner, get married or have kids: these are all goals. They can be ticked off the list: 'Done!' Values, in contrast, are how you want to behave every step of the way as you move towards your goals; how you want to behave when you achieve your goals; and how you want to behave when you *don't* achieve your goals!

For example, if your values are to be loving, kind and caring, then you can behave in these ways right now and forever — even if you never achieve the goal of finding a partner or having kids. And, of course, you *could* achieve those goals of having a partner and kids, but neglect to be kind, loving and caring. Similarly, if in the workplace your values are to be productive, efficient, sociable, attentive and responsible, you can behave in these ways right now, even if your job 'totally sucks'. And, you *could* have a great job, but neglect all those aforementioned values.

Now suppose you want to be loved or respected: are those values? No, they are goals! They are all about trying to get something — in this case trying to get love or respect from others. Your values are how *you* want to behave as you pursue those goals, regardless of whether you achieve them or not. Now if you want to be loving or respectful, those *are* values; they are desired qualities of behaviour and we can act lovingly or respectfully to ourselves or to others whenever we choose to. But to be loved or respected are goals (or 'wants' or 'needs') and they are out of our control; we can't make someone love us or respect us. In fact, the more we try to make someone love us or respect us, the less likely they are to do so! But if we act lovingly and respectfully towards ourselves and others, there's a good chance we will be loved and respected in return. (No guarantees, of course; unlike fairytales, life doesn't always give us a happy ending.)

What about rules, then? How do we distinguish rules from values? Well, rules can usually be identified by words such as 'right', 'wrong', 'good', 'bad', 'should', 'shouldn't', 'have to', 'must' and 'ought'. Rules tell you how to live your life: the right and wrong way of doing things. Values do *not* do this; values simply describe the qualities you wish to bring to your ongoing behaviour. So 'Thou shalt not kill' is *not* a value; it is a rule. It tells you what you should and shouldn't do; what is right and wrong. The values underneath this rule are caring (for human life) and respect (for human life).

Of course, we can use our values to help set rules that guide us, but we do need to be clear that they are not one and the same thing. Values give us a sense of freedom because there are so many different ways in which we can act on them. In contrast, rules often give us a sense of restriction or obligation; they often weigh us down and limit our options. Suppose we help someone out because we're consciously in touch with our values: we wish to be kind and generous. Now compare this to helping someone out because we're fused with rigid rules: 'it's the right thing to do', or we 'should do it', or we 'owe them', or we 'are obliged to'. The former approach tends to be freeing and energising; the latter is often restrictive, draining and burdensome.

Values, goals and rules are all very important and we can make good use of all of them in our lives — but we do need to keep in mind their differences, as we use them in different ways for different ends. For example, we can use our values to set goals, to guide our actions, and to help us create useful rules (such as ethics and morals and codes of conduct).

So what has all this got to do with the reality gap? Well, once we have dropped anchor, we need to take action; to stand for something in the face of all our pain. There is no fulfilment to be found in giving up. So when life asks us the question: 'What will you stand for?' we can find the answer in our values: 'I will stand for being the person I truly want to be; I will stand for acting on what matters, deep in my heart.' And through this response, we infuse our life with purpose. We give ourselves something to live for. We give life meaning.

If this still doesn't make much sense to you, or you get the concept but you're not quite sure what your own values actually are . . . then, yes, you guessed it, that's normal. So in the next chapter, there's a little exercise for you, which I'm pretty sure will make it all clear. In the meantime, reflect further on the list of big questions on page 132 and see if there's any link between the answers you come up with and these words of the British scientist, Sir Humphry Davy:

Life is made up, not of great sacrifices or duties, but of little things, in which smiles, and kindnesses, and small obligations, given habitually, are what win and preserve the heart and secure comfort.

Intention 4 breathing sessions.
4 I am finding a strong sense
purpose in life".

Chapter 15

PURPOSE AND PAIN

Life is both kind and cruel; it doles out both wonder and dread
in generous serves. In my years as a GP, I met many people who
had suffered terribly in life. I saw children disfigured by fire and
babies with fatal diseases. I saw strong capable adults reduced
to invalids and brilliant minds wiped away by dementia. I saw
bodies misshaped and deformed through all manner of injury
— the victims of violence and disaster. I saw refugees from
foreign lands, struggling to rebuild their lives after rape and
torture, or struggling to start again after losing most of their
family. I saw the freshly bereaved, howling in their anguish;
distraught mothers clutching their still-born babies. I saw men
with weeping sores and blistering skin, and women with broken
bones and bleeding arteries. I saw the blind, the deaf and the
paralysed, the seriously ill and the newly deceased.

And in the midst of all this pain, I saw courage, kindness and
compassion. I saw people reaching out and helping each other;
families bonding through crisis; friends and neighbours holding
each other's hands. I saw men and women facing death with
dignity; love and affection pouring from broken hearts. I saw
parents slowly rebuilding shattered lives, finding the strength
within to persist and grow.

It never ceases to amaze me that in the midst of great pain

we find great passion. A terrible crisis frequently brings out the best in us. It prompts us to open our hearts and search within — to reach inside and discover what we are made of.

Now, obviously, none of us likes or wants a reality gap. Indeed, the greater it is, the more intensely we dislike it, and the more desperately we want to get rid of it. But we can all make a choice about how we respond to it, and at times of great crisis many of us surprise ourselves. We may doubt ourselves or blame ourselves, but still rise bravely to the occasion and discover courage and strength in abundant supply.

Sadly, many of us only find these inner resources when reality knocks us over and stamps on our head. So why wait until that happens? Why not get in touch with our hearts right now and get clear about what we want to stand for in life, so we can align our actions to a chosen purpose? That way, when the reality gap opens wide (and it will) we can be prepared for it. This preparation is important, because when we have a strong sense of purpose in life, it is easier to make peace with a reality gap and make room for the pain that goes with it; it enables us to find vitality through taking meaningful action, despite all the pain. Without a sense of purpose, we can easily give up on life when the pain gets too great; we lose hope, 'fall into a heap' or put our life on hold. But if we take the time to infuse our life with meaning, we are far less likely to give up on it when the going gets tough.

Now as I mentioned earlier, when I ask my clients about meaning, purpose or values, they commonly become anxious, confused or go blank. At that point, I often take them through an exercise called 'The Sweet Spot', which was created by one of my mentors, the brilliant psychologist Kelly Wilson. I invite you now to try a simplified version of this exercise.

The Sweet Spot

First, retrieve a memory — it could be a recent one, or one from the distant past — which encapsulates some of life's sweetness for you. (Yes, even though life serves up much sorrow and pain, it also serves up much that is rich and sweet.) This memory does not have to be dramatic. It could be something momentous, such as skiing in the Swiss Alps, hiking through the Himalayas, holding your newborn baby in your arms, or having mad passionate sex with the love of your life. Or it *could* also be something as simple as sitting in a café and reading the paper while sipping your freshly brewed coffee, or riding your bike through the park on a sunny afternoon, or playing tennis with a friend, or reading a book on a beach, or having a hug with a loved one, or playing your favourite music. Literally anything that captures a taste of life's richness will do.

Now close your eyes and make that memory as vivid as possible, as if it is happening here and now. See if you can tap right into the sweetness; to drink it in and let it flow through you; to appreciate the fullness of life as it was in that moment. And you may well find as you do this, that the sweetness of this memory is mixed with pain. You may encounter some sadness, longing or regret. This is hardly surprising, because whatever we hold precious will usually bring us pain. So as you engage with this memory, be open and make room for all that arises: the sweetness *and* the sorrow; the pleasure *and* the pain.

When you reach the end of this paragraph, put the book down, straighten your spine, let your shoulders drop and push your feet gently on to the floor. Close your eyes and take a few slow, deep breaths. Once you are calm and centred, relive your chosen memory in vivid detail. Take at least a minute or two, or longer if you wish. And as you relive this memory, look around inside it and explore it and notice what you can see, hear, touch, taste and smell. And really savour that sweetness — really let yourself feel it, and as you do so, make room for all that arises.

* * *

So how did you find that? Did you find it enjoyable? Did sadness or other painful emotions arise? If so, did you open up and make room for them? That was actually just the first part of the exercise. The second part is to go back into that memory, take a good look at yourself and:

Notice, *inside that memory*, what are you doing?

Notice, *inside that memory*, how are you behaving?

Notice, *inside that memory*, what personal qualities you are exhibiting?

Notice, *inside that memory*, the nature of your relationship with whatever activity you are doing: are you connected or disconnected; engaged or disengaged?

Notice, *inside that memory*, how are you treating yourself, others, and the world around you?

Then ponder the following questions for at least a
few minutes:

What does this reveal about the personal qualities
you'd like to embody?

What does this suggest about the way you'd ideally
like to behave?

The Three C's

From an ACT perspective, there is no such thing as a 'right' or
'wrong' value. For example, suppose you wish to be loving,
caring, spontaneous, generous, supportive, sensual or forgiving:
those values are not 'right' in any objective sense. Your social
group may well judge your values and if the consensus is
that they are 'good' they are then called 'virtues'. But values
themselves can't be 'right' or 'wrong', any more than our
taste in pizza, ice-cream or wine can be 'right' or 'wrong'. Like
our taste in food and drink, our values simply express our
preferences: they describe how we wish to behave on an ongoing
basis.

Because of this, no ACT coach or therapist would ever dream
of telling you what values to live by — only you can make that
choice for yourself. However, I would like to share some
information with you in the hope that it might help you clarify
what your values are. You see, I've questioned thousands of
people about their values and, while they come up with dozens
of different words, their answers usually fall under three main
headings: Connection, Caring and Contribution. And I'm
willing to bet that your 'sweet memory' involves some or all of
these three values. So let me ask you:

In this memory, are you deeply _connected_ (i.e. engaged or
fully present with someone, something or some activity)? Are

you connected with another person, or with some miracle of nature, or with some type of food or drink or art or music? Are you connected with some activity: whether it is physical, mental or creative? Are you connected with your body, mind or spirit?

And within this memory, are you *caring* about someone, something or some activity? Is your heart wide open? Are you in touch with something that matters to you? Are you expressing concern or affection for yourself or others? Are you treating someone or something as precious or important?

And in this memory, are you *contributing* to someone or something? Are you contributing to your own health and happiness? Are you contributing to others and either supporting, nurturing, helping or loving them? Are you looking after nature or taking care of the environment? Or are you looking after your body, mind or spirit? Are you creating something for others to appreciate, or contributing to a team, group or community? Are you sharing something special with a loved one? Are you reaching out with kindness, warmth or tenderness? Are you contributing love, enthusiasm, curiosity, courage or creativity?

* * *

I must confess that I am feeling quite nervous as I write this section of the book. This is because, as I said earlier, in ACT we do not tell you which values to choose, but offer all sorts of exercises to help you clarify your own values. (You'll find such an exercise in Appendix 3.) Therefore, let me say once again, the three C's are not the 'right' values, or the 'best' ones, or the 'proper' ones, and there is no need to agree with them or embrace them as your own. However, the three C's *are* very common and many people find them useful as a starting point for living life with purpose. (This is why you'll repeatedly encounter them in virtually all spiritual, religious and personal development pathways, across many societies, in virtually every period of human history.)

Now obviously there are many human values. (Indeed, you'll find a list of fifty-eight common values in the aforementioned exercise in Appendix 3!) However, if you look closely, you'll find that almost all values grow from within the soil of the three C's. For example, values such as love, compassion, kindness, honesty, intimacy, trust, creativity, authenticity, openness, forgiveness and courage all have their roots in connection, caring and contribution. To help make this clear, let's take a look at the roots of love.

The Three Pillars of Love

When you hear the word 'love' what springs to mind? Most people think of it as a feeling: a blissful emotion that floods your heart with joy. But we can also think of love as an action. For example, when we say 'she is a very loving person', we are not referring to her feelings, we are referring to the manner in which she acts: her words, her deeds and her gestures. And if we wish to love well — to love anyone or anything, including ourselves — we will need the three C's to do so.

For example, consider the love of a parent for a child. If you want to be a loving parent, then *feeling* love for your child is hardly enough. There are plenty of parents in the world who have *feelings* of love for their children, but neglect or abuse them. To be a loving parent, you need to *act* with love.

You need to *connect* with your child: to engage with him or her and be psychologically present. (If you are distracted or disengaged and not paying attention, then what message are you sending?)

And you need to *care* about your child: to care about his or her health, wellbeing and happiness; to understand his or her fears, passions and dreams, the way he or she sees the world, and his or her hopes for the future. (If you are uncaring, then what message are you sending?)

You need to *contribute* to this child: to actively nurture and support him or her; to help and encourage him or her; to soothe and reassure him or her; to give kindness, understanding and affection; to give time, energy and attention. (If you contribute little or nothing, then what message are you sending?)

Hopefully you can see that connection, caring and contribution are the three pillars of love, not just if we wish to be loving towards a child, but also if we want to be loving towards a partner, a parent, a pet, a project, a friend, a relative, a hobby, an activity, the environment, the planet or ourselves. And if you explore other values in a similar way, again and again you'll find the three C's at their root.

Purpose and Relationships

Suppose we think of our life as a huge and complex network of relationships: relationships with our body and mind; relationships with our family, friends and colleagues; relationships with our work and environment; and so on. If we want to live with purpose — to stand for something that matters — this idea is a very useful starting point. It enables us to let go of unhelpful stories such as 'Life has no meaning', or 'I don't know what to do with my life', or 'Is this all there is?' Instead, we acknowledge that our life — no matter how wonderful or dreadful it may be — is a rich tapestry of relationships, and our purpose is to make them as good as possible.

If you agree with this proposition, then here is all you need to do, in any moment, to infuse your life with purpose: choose a relationship that matters and help it to flourish. And what might that involve? You guessed it: connection, caring and contribution. Let's talk this through.

Connection

If we want to make the most of any relationship, we need to connect: to engage, to participate, to be fully present; to be conscious, open and involved. When we connect fully with anyone or anything, the relationship is far richer than when we are disconnected or 'absent-minded'.

Caring

There is little hope for a relationship if we do not care. When we truly care about a relationship, and we act in ways that are caring, the relationship thrives. But if we act in ways that are hostile, uncaring or neglectful, the relationship withers.

Contribution

To help a relationship flourish, we need to contribute: to support, to help out, to provide, to give, to nurture, to care, to share. If we don't give to the relationship, it will suffer.

***

To make this clear, let's look at three different relationships. First consider your relationship with this book. Are you connecting with the words? Are you engaging in the experience of reading? Do you care about what you read? Do you care about the difference it could make to your life? Are you contributing enthusiasm or curiosity? Now consider this: have you ever had a relationship with a book where you *didn't* connect with the words, or you *didn't* care about the content, or you *didn't* contribute enthusiasm or curiosity? If so, was it rewarding and fulfilling, or did it feel like a waste of your time?

Next consider self-compassion: a relationship with yourself.

Clearly it is based on all three C's: you are connecting with yourself, caring about yourself and contributing kindness to yourself.

Last but not least, consider defusion and expansion. In practising these skills, we are building better relationships with our thoughts and feelings. We care about them: we care about what they mean and how they affect us. We also connect with them: we notice where they are and what they are doing and what they look like, sound like or feel like. And we contribute to them: we give them space, we offer them peace and we contribute our curiosity.

* * *

The great thing with this approach is that we can *instantly* make our life more meaningful — we don't have to wait until we find some noble cause or life mission, we can simply bring the three C's into any or all of our relationships, here and now. In the next chapter, we'll look at how to do that, but in the meantime, let's finish with something to reflect on: a quote from the Canadian poet, Henry Drummond:

You will find, as you look back upon your life, that the moments when you have really lived are the moments when you have done things in the spirit of love.

Chapter 16

WHAT REALLY COUNTS?

Have you ever heard this saying: 'It's the thought that counts'?

Let's think about this for a moment. Which means more to you: when someone has a thought about buying you a birthday present, or when they actually go out and buy you one? Which of these will get you into trouble with the law: if you have thoughts about committing a crime, or if you actually go out and commit one? Which will count the most to your children: if you think about being a loving and supportive parent, or if you actually are loving and supportive? No child has ever said: 'What I really admired about my Dad was that although he was totally selfish and was never there for me when I needed him, he often *thought* about being more caring and giving.'

So let's face it: it's our actions that count, not our thoughts. And it's just as well, or we'd all be in a lot of trouble. Think of all those angry, vengeful thoughts you've had in your life; of all those times you've thought of doing something to hurt another person, such as yelling offensive insults or saying nasty put-downs, or committing acts of revenge. And have you ever had thoughts about leaving your partner, or having sex with someone else? (If not, you're very unusual; almost everybody in a long-term relationship has thoughts like this at times.) And that's not the half of it. The fact is that we all have plenty of thoughts that we would be deeply embarrassed to admit to in public. So what state would our lives be in if these thoughts really did count more than our actions?

We create our life through our actions, not through our thoughts. One of my current clients has been seriously thinking about quitting his dull, tedious, undemanding job and retraining as a psychologist. The problem is, he's been thinking about it seriously for more than ten years — and he still hasn't taken any action! And isn't he a bit like you and me? Most of us spend far too much time thinking about what we want to do with our time on this planet, but nowhere near enough time actually doing it.

Of course, usually when we say, 'It's the thought that counts', it serves a specific purpose: we are trying to make somebody else feel better. We suspect they are feeling bad because they haven't followed through on something they considered important (such as buying that birthday present), and we want to let them off the hook. So next time you're in this situation, why not say something that serves the same purpose, but is a bit more genuine and compassionate, such as: 'Ah, well. You're only human. I do things like that too. Really, it's no big deal.'

And next time you're *thinking* about an important or meaningful area of your life, why not ask yourself these questions: 'What's a tiny step I could take? What's the smallest, easiest, simplest action I could do to make a difference in this part of my life?' After all, when it comes to creating the life you want, even the tiniest actions count for more than many hundreds of hours of thinking.

This is where the three C's can really help us. We all have so many different values, we can easily get lost inside our minds, trying to analyse our way to a life of purpose. But the three C's can help us to step out of our thoughts and get into action, whenever we wish, no matter what we are doing. All we need to do is ask ourselves two simple questions:

- What relationship matters most in this moment?
- What could I do, right now, in this relationship that involves connection, caring or contribution?

Let's look at a few examples to tease this out. Suppose the relationship that matters most to you in this moment is the one with your own thoughts and feelings. Could you connect with them: notice where they are, what they are doing, and how you are responding to them? Could you care about them: acknowledge they have an important role in your life; that they are telling you something important about what matters to you? Could you contribute peace and space and openness and curiosity?

Suppose the relationship that matters most right now is with your body. Could you connect with it and be curious? How does it feel? What is it doing? How is it moving? Where is it tense and where is it relaxed? Where is it strong and where is it weak? What makes it function better and what makes it worse? Could you care for and contribute to your body through stretching, or exercise, or eating well, or sleeping well, or giving it a rest, or teaching it a new skill, or taking it for a walk in the park? ~~Transformational Breath~~

And if the most important relationship is with your mind, could you connect with it and notice what it's up to? Is it doing something useful? Is it fantasising, remembering, worrying, pondering or planning? If you wanted to care and contribute, could you give your mind a rest? Or could you teach it a new skill? Or could you introduce it to something interesting such as some new books, music or movies?

And if the most important relationship in this moment is with your art, or your sport, or your hobby, or your work, or

Full immersion.

your study, then what happens when you *connect* with it; when you immerse your full attention to the task and let distracting thoughts come and go? And what happens to this relationship when you *contribute*; when you give it your enthusiasm, curiosity, courage, creativity or patience? And what happens to this relationship when you are *caring*: when you take time to appreciate it, or you act with greater care and consideration?

And if this relationship happens to be with a person, then the same three questions apply, regardless of whether that person is your partner, child, parent, friend, neighbour, teacher, student, mentor, customer, employer or co-worker. How can you connect with them with openness and curiosity? You might pay more attention to their face, their tone of voice, their body posture, or the words that they are saying. What can you do to show that you care? You might be curious about their emotions, their thoughts, or their beliefs, attitudes and assumptions and try to understand their world and their needs. What can you do to contribute to their life? This doesn't have to be big or dramatic; the smallest act of kindness or caring will do.

Of course, if this other person is treating you badly, you'll need to shift your priorities within this relationship. First and foremost, you'll need to take care of and contribute to *your own* health and wellbeing; to do what is necessary to protect and look after yourself and meet your own needs. And if the bad treatment persists, you may well wish to consider ending the relationship. (Of course, this is not always possible, but even if it is, it may not be the best option. For example, if you're caring for a loved one who has some sort of illness that leads them to be abusive.) Either way, while the relationship persists, your priority should be caring for yourself within it.

I hope by now you can see the three C's are vital for every relationship: with people or pets, with God or science, with art, nature or technology. For example, consider the case of Rob, a

22-year-old university student. Rob was studying a five-year architecture course and he worked part-time as a waiter to help pay his way. He told me that he hated his job, but he needed the money to pay for his food and board. He knew it was only temporary — that in one more year he'd be working as an architect — but that didn't stop him from dreading every shift. And it wasn't that he worked in a horrible place or had some terrible boss; he just didn't like the work. And the only other part-time work he could get was cleaning, stocking shelves, serving hamburgers or bartending, and these were, in his opinion, even worse.

So I questioned him about the three C's and how he could use them to transform his relationship with his job. What might happen if he *connected* more with the customers? What difference might it make if he were to be fully present? To pay attention with openness and curiosity to the clothes they wore, the style of their hair, and the tone and rhythm of their voices? To notice the way that they ate and drank and spoke? To notice their facial expressions and physical gestures?

And what might happen if he *cared* more about the customers: if he cared about their experience in the restaurant and the quality of his service? Inspired by this way of thinking, Rob had an idea. He would become a 'Zen master of pizza delivery'. He would *connect* with his body to ensure he had the best possible posture and carry that pizza as if it were a priceless work of art. He would *care* about how he lowered that pizza to the table; he'd lay it down as if placing it in front of a king. And all the while, he would *contribute* warmth and good grace and he'd also share his excellent sense of humour.

And the result? Well, his work didn't magically turn into some 'dream job', but it did become much more fulfilling. He wasn't 'just waiting pizzas' anymore; now he was contributing to people's lives, challenging his body, engaging in the world, developing his mindfulness skills, and having moments of fun along the way. He was staggered by the difference it made. The dread disappeared and so did the boredom. He hadn't closed the reality gap — there was still a huge difference between the job he ideally wanted and the one he had — but he had discovered the fulfilment of living with purpose.

Chapter 17

THE FOUR APPROACHES

You can't cross the sea merely by standing and staring at the water. — Rabindranath Tagore

So there I stood, facing a gap so huge it was more like a chasm. My beautiful son, just two years old, had been tagged with a spine-chilling diagnosis: autism. My mind and body were flooded with shock and fear. Now that I was present and treating myself with compassion, what on earth was I going to do next?

When reality hits us hard, we tend to retreat. This is only to be expected; it's what comes naturally. We use what methods we know to try to escape — anything from movies and music to drinking and drugs. And even if we escape for only a moment, the relief is huge. However, a life lived in retreat is not fulfilling. And if we spend our days in a constant fight with reality, we will soon be exhausted. So if we want to thrive in the face of a huge reality gap, we have no choice but to stand for something in the face of it; to open ourselves to life as it is in this moment, and stand for something that matters deep in our heart.

The capacity for humans to live rich and meaningful lives in

the midst of great adversity is often referred to as 'resilience'.
There is a wealth of scientific research on resilience but we can
boil most of it down to a simple formula, which I have
appropriately labelled 'The Resilience Formula'.

The Resilience Formula: Four Approaches
to Any Problematic Situation

In any problematic situation, there are four possible approaches
to consider:

- Leave the situation.
- Stay, and change what can be changed.
- Stay, and accept what can't be changed, and live by your
  values.
- Stay, and give up trying, and do things that make the
  situation worse.

Let's take a look at each in turn.

1. Leave the Situation

To leave the situation is not always an option. For example, if
you happen to be in prison, you can't just walk away. But, very
often, leaving the situation *is* an option. If you're in a lousy
marriage, or a lousy job, or a lousy neighbourhood, then it's
worth considering: would your overall quality of life be better if
you left than if you stayed? Of course, you can never know this
for certain, but you can make a reasonable prediction based on
what has happened up to this point.

2. Stay, and Change What Can Be Changed

You may discount option one for all sorts of reasons. For

example, some people, no matter how bad their marriage may be, are unwilling to break their wedding vows. They *could* leave, but they choose not to. So if you choose to stay in a difficult situation (or if you have no choice but to stay), then do whatever you possibly can to improve it. In other words, if there's any way to close this reality gap (without creating new ones that are even bigger) then take action to close it.

Clearly there are some reality gaps we *can't* close, like the death of a loved one, or a permanent disability. But many reality gaps *can* be closed — at least to some degree. If we're unfit or overweight, if we've got a treatable illness, if we're neglecting our family or friends, if we have an addiction, or if we're in a financial crisis: these are gaps we *can* do something about. And, of course, there are some reality gaps where we just don't know what is possible — where we can't know for certain whether they can or can't be closed. In these cases, the only way to find out is to try our best to close them and see what happens.

Now whether the gap can or can't be closed, we are still faced with the necessity of action; for as long as we're still breathing, life goes on. So the choice then is, do we actively choose the direction we wish to take, or do we passively go along for the ride? Not surprisingly, the greatest vitality lies in choosing to act in line with our deepest values; to steer our life forwards in some meaningful direction.

So, how do we do this? We use our values to help us set some goals. We set short-term, medium-term and long-term goals to get us closer to the life we want to live. (Note: To set goals effectively is quite a skill, and most of us are not naturally good at it. So if you'd like some help with this, go to Appendix 4, which will guide you step-by-step through the process.) Then once we've set some goals, we take action!

Alas, we can't know in advance if we'll achieve our goals, but we *can* start taking action right away. And the moment we do, we will experience a sense of empowerment and vitality; a sense of embracing life and making the most of it, instead of letting it pass us by.

3. Stay, and Accept What Can't Be Changed, and Live By Your Values

If you've chosen to stay (or you have to), and you've taken every action possible to improve the situation, then practise acceptance. Accept all those painful feelings: open up and make room for them. Accept that your mind will have lots to say that's unhelpful: defuse from all those harsh judgements and self-defeating stories and give them plenty of space to come, stay, and go in their own good time. Pull yourself out of the smog and engage in the present. Choose to live by your values and engage fully in life, irrespective of the challenges you face.

(Note: Options two and three generally occur simultaneously. I have listed them in this order to emphasise the importance of taking action. Also keep in mind that if you *do* choose option one (i.e. to leave), then *as you leave*, practise options two and three: change what can be changed, accept what can't be changed, and live by your values.)

4. Stay, and Give Up Trying, and Do Things That Make the Situation Worse

We've all chosen option four at times in our lives. Most of us do it repeatedly! All too often we stay in a problematic situation, but we *don't* do everything possible to improve it, *nor* do we practise acceptance and living by our values. Instead, we do things that make the situation worse — we may worry, ruminate and blame; we may pace up and down, kick the wall, yell and rant and cry; we may turn to drugs or alcohol or even double-coated chocolate Tim Tams! We may pick quarrels with our

loved ones, or wear them down with our complaining, hopelessness or bitterness. We may withdraw from the world, lie in bed,
or zone out in front of the TV. We may put our life on hold
and let the problem consume all our waking moments. We may
even resort to self-harm or suicide. And all this does is suck
the life right out of us. There is no fulfilment to be found in
option four.

Cancerian***

The life of Nelson Mandela gives an excellent example of the
resilience formula in action. For twenty-seven years, he was
imprisoned by the South African government. Why? Because he
dared to fight for freedom and democracy; to oppose apartheid,
the official government policy of racial discrimination. Now
when you look at his reality gap during those years, option one
was clearly out: he couldn't *leave* prison. And option two was
out for most of the time: there was very little he could do to
improve his living conditions. So mostly, he chose option three.
He accepted his painful thoughts and feelings, engaged in the
present, and lived by his values: standing for freedom, equality
and peace. For instance, during his first seventeen years in
prison, on Robben Island, Mandela had to do hard labour in a
lime quarry. But he turned the situation to his advantage. You
see, Mandela knew that education was essential for equality and
democracy, so he arranged illegal meetings in the tunnels of the
quarry — educational sessions, where the more educated
prisoners would teach and instruct the others. (Later this came
to be known as 'Mandela University'.)

One of the most remarkable aspects of Mandela's story is
that in 1985, after twenty-two years in prison, the South African
government offered to release him — but he turned them down!
Why? Because the condition for release was that he would have
to remain silent; that he would refrain from speaking out against

apartheid. Naturally, for Mandela to do this, he would have had to go against his core values, so he chose to stay in prison instead. That meant *another five years in prison* before he finally received release without this condition! And yet, despite this huge reality gap, he was able to find fulfilment in standing for something: freedom, democracy and equality.

Mandela's case is extraordinary, but the formula applies to each and every one of us, no matter what our situation is. For instance, if your job or your marriage is 'terrible', consider leaving. If you choose to stay, do everything you can to improve it. If it's still 'terrible', accept what can't be changed — including all those unpleasant thoughts and feelings that are certain to arise — and live by your values: be the person you want to be and stand for something in the face of this reality gap.

When I present these options to my clients, most of them feel empowered: it helps them to realise they have choices. However, from time to time, someone has a strong negative reaction: usually a mixture of anger and anxiety. Why should this be? Usually it's because they find it too confronting. The resilience formula confronts us with the reality that we have choices and therefore we are responsible for how we act. There is short-term relief in option four: in buying the story that it's all too hard, that we may as well give up, and we are powerless, but the relief this can bring doesn't last. In the long term, this option drains the life from us. Our vitality lies only in taking a stand: in choosing options one, two or three. However, we will only experience this vitality if we take our stand with a quality known as 'willingness'.

What does 'willingness' mean? Well, psychologist Hank Robb explains it as follows. Suppose you hand over ten pounds for a ticket to the cinema. You can give the money resentfully or grudgingly, or you can give the money willingly, but either way, you still have to hand over the money. And when you pay it willingly, the experience is far more fulfilling than if you do so resentfully.

So when we take a stand, let's do so willingly. If we take this stand fused with 'I have no choice', or 'I hate having to do this', or 'I shouldn't have to do this', or 'This is my lot in life', or 'I have to do it; it's my duty', we will feel burdened, disempowered or drained. Remember, there is no 'have to', 'must', 'ought' or 'should' in a value; such words just turn our values into life-draining rules.

So if you feel drained or burdened or resentful as you take a stand, then notice what unhelpful story has hooked you. Then unhook yourself from it and come back to your values and recognise that you *do* have a choice. You can *choose* to stand for something — or not. You certainly don't *have to*. The big question is, are you *willing* to? Ask yourself: 'Am I *willing* to take a stand in the face of this gap? Am I *willing* to act with purpose, even if painful thoughts and feelings arise?'

You may wonder how I applied the resilience formula when my son was first diagnosed with autism. Well, I discounted option one immediately. I'd heard many sad stories of parents who abandoned their children; no way would I become one of them! And as for option four: well as you know, that *was* my initial response, but it just made things harder.

So once I'd dropped anchor, I was left with options two and three: change what can be changed, accept what can't be changed, and live by my values. And that's exactly what I did. The values I chose to live by were love, patience, persistence, courage and compassion. And guided by these values, I set out to change whatever I could; to close the reality gap as much as possible.

I scoured the Internet and contacted a variety of professionals to find out what could be done for this condition. The problem is, when it comes to autism (or any other disorder, for that matter!) so many people make so many claims about their treatments, it is overwhelming. Websites tout a vast number of approaches, and charismatic professionals not only swear by their methods, but provide all sorts of inspiring anecdotes of the many individuals who have benefited. So how can you possibly know what the best course of action should be? Well, the inconvenient truth is that you can't know for sure. You have to make a choice.

So what, then, do you base your choice on? My wife and I based our choice on the best available scientific evidence. We soon discovered that there is only one scientifically proven approach that creates significant, lasting, positive changes — without medication — in the majority of children who undertake it. This approach is called ABA (Applied Behaviour Analysis), and it involves training the autistic child in all the skills they are lacking: thinking skills, language/communication skills, play skills, social skills and attention skills — basically 'rewiring the brain' to function more normally. (For more information on ABA, turn to Appendix 5.)

We also discovered that the best-researched ABA programme available, the 'Lovaas Programme', involves a team of therapists working one-on-one with the child for thirty to forty hours a week, over a period of three to four years. This presented us with a dilemma. Imagine a two-year-old child working six hours a day, five days a week, having to painstakingly learn these essential skills. That's a huge demand to place on a little child! Could we really impose this burden on our little boy? The programme also places huge demands on the parents because they have to do much of the work themselves, outside of 'therapy hours'. So my wife and I struggled mightily with the decision. We had a huge amount of anxiety. What if it didn't work? What if it was all too much for our son to handle? What if it was all too much for *us* to handle?

However, ultimately we made room for our fear, and we enrolled our son in an excellent ABA programme in Melbourne (called *Learning For Life*) and within the very first *day* of his treatment, we noticed significant improvements. And thereafter, things moved very rapidly. Within the space of just a few weeks, our little boy's vocabulary increased from ten words to over a hundred; he started to make good eye contact, he learned his own name, and he started to understand more of what we were saying.

We were ecstatic.

Of course, we were extremely lucky in many ways. For a start, in many parts of the world, ABA is not available. And even when it is available, many people can't afford the full treatment; it is very expensive! And of course, not all children respond as well as my son did.

However, even though we were fortunate, it wasn't as if all our dreams had come true. The reality gap had certainly started to close a little, but it was still pretty huge. Our son had all sorts of problems, not just cognitively, but also physically: he had significant deficits in his balance, coordination, muscle strength, motor skills; and at this point, he still wasn't even walking! And my wife and I also had plenty of problems: we had the financial stress of paying for the treatment, the emotional stress of the Lovaas Programme itself, our ongoing grief and fear and, last but not least, the enormous toll of all this stress upon our marriage. (I do not find it surprising that the divorce rates are sky-high for parents of children with disabilities.)

And then we discovered something that ramped up our stress even higher. We found out that there was a new type of ABA programme, based on something called RFT (Relational Frame Theory). Now I was already familiar with RFT: it is the theory of behaviour and cognition that underlies ACT, but what I didn't know back then is that RFT has profound implications for the treatment of autism. It would take too long to explain the how and why of it, so let's just say that RFT dramatically speeds up ABA programmes and leads to better outcomes in much less time. (If you want to know more about it, turn to Appendix 5.)

So why did this discovery stress us out? Because there was only one such programme in Australia and it was on the other side of the continent from where we lived: in the world's most isolated city — Perth.

So we dithered and fretted and debated: should we move or not? To pack up everything and relocate to a city where we knew absolutely no one: was it really worth it? After all, our son was making very good progress. His ABA programme in Melbourne was truly excellent. Did we really need to move?

And yet . . . if RFT could really make a difference; if it could get better results than traditional ABA, then how could we deprive our son of that opportunity?

So we did, eventually, pack up and move to Perth. And it proved to be extremely stressful in many ways. But no matter how hard it got, or how much it hurt, my wife and I knew we were standing for something important. We knew that whatever the outcome, we would be able to look back and say, 'We didn't quit. We didn't lose hope. We did everything we possibly could to help him.' And that, in itself, was deeply fulfilling.

Luckily, that move to Perth turned out for the best. Our son excelled in the new programme under the care of psychologist Darin Cairns. His language skills, social skills and comprehension skills improved at a rate that astonished us. We had planned to be in Perth for three years, but after eighteen months the programme came to an end. Why? Because our son had improved so much *he no longer met the diagnostic criteria for autism.* To see that happy four-and-a-half-year-old boy running around the kindergarten, chatting with the other kids, and laughing and joining in their games: it seemed like a miracle. Hard to believe that at age two, this same little boy could not walk, could barely talk, and didn't even know his own name.

However, although it may have seemed like a miracle, it wasn't. It was the result of lots of very hard work: a result of committed action, guided by values. And there is still a hard road ahead for us because although our son is no longer autistic — not by any stretch of the imagination — he still has ongoing issues, such as learning difficulties, high anxiety levels, and social difficulties. But whenever it all seems too much, I drop anchor and come back to my values. And I remember what I want to stand for as a father: love, patience, persistence, courage and compassion. And when I consciously choose to act on those values, the tiniest little action is loaded with purpose.

Footnote: I do not want this book to be taken over by a discussion of treatments for autism, but as I write this, I can't help thinking that some of my readers are undoubtedly parents of autistic children, and they may well have reactions of envy or resentment or other painful emotions upon reading about my son's outcome. If this is the case for you, please keep in mind that it is completely natural to have such emotional reactions. So go gently on yourself. Make room for the pain, and hold yourself kindly. These emotions simply show how much you care for your own child.

Chapter 18

HOLDING HOT COALS

Do you ever get caught up in resentment? Many of us do, especially after a major reality slap. We may resent others because they let us down, they treated us badly, they didn't care about us, they achieved more than us, they're 'better off' than us, or for dozens of other reasons. Resentment is a particularly sticky version of the 'not good enough' story; a version heavily infused with anger, righteousness and a strong sense of injustice.

When we get hooked by resentment, it almost always pulls us into self-defeating struggles. In Buddhism they say: 'Resentment is like grasping a red hot coal in order to throw it at someone else.' At Alcoholics Anonymous (AA) they say: 'Resentment is like swallowing poison and hoping the other person dies.' What these sayings have in common is the idea that when we get hooked by resentment, all we do is hurt ourselves even more than we already are.

Resentment comes from the French word *resentir*, which means 'to feel again'. This makes sense: each time resentment hooks us we *feel again* our hurt, our anger, and our sense of unfairness or injustice. The events that happened are now in the past, but as we dwell on them in the present, we *feel again* all that pain. And as we stew in our anger and dissatisfaction, all our vitality seeps away.

A somewhat similar story is self-blame, which we can think of as resentment turned on ourselves. Again and again our minds remind us of all the things we did wrong, then we get angry and judge or punish ourselves. We *feel again* all our pain, regret, angst, disappointment and anxiety. And, of course, this does not alter the past in any way, nor does it enable us to learn and grow from our mistakes. Again, all we achieve is to hurt ourselves more.

So what is the antidote to resentment and self-blame? Forgiveness — but not forgiveness as we commonly think of it. In the ACT model, forgiveness does *not* mean forgetting. Nor does it mean that what happened was okay, or excusable, or trivial, or unimportant. And nor does it involve saying or doing anything to someone else.

To understand the ACT notion of forgiveness, let's consider the origin of the word. 'Forgive' is derived from two separate words: 'give' and 'before'. So in ACT, forgiveness simply means this: giving yourself back what was there before the 'bad stuff' happened. At some point in the past — and it may have been recent, or it may have been a long time ago — something very painful happened. Either *you* did something that you now blame yourself for, or *others* did something that you now resent them for. And since that time, your mind has repeatedly pulled you back to those events, getting you to feel all the pain, again and again.

So what was your life like *before* those events happened? Were you getting on with life and making the most of it? Were you living in the present? Even if your life *wasn't* very good before all these events took place, at least you weren't lost in the choking smog of resentment or self-blame. So how about giving yourself back the clarity and freedom of life without all that smog? You see, in the ACT model, forgiveness has nothing to do with anybody else; it is something you do purely for yourself. It's *giving* yourself back what was there *before*: a life free from the burden of resentment or self-blame.

How do we cultivate this type of forgiveness? You already have all the knowledge and skills you need. When our minds generate stories that tend to feed resentment or self-blame, our first steps are to notice them and name them. We could say to ourselves something like, 'Here's my mind beating up on me' or 'Here's a painful memory from the past' or 'Here's my mind judging other people' or 'Here's my mind pulling me into a struggle'. At the same time, we hold ourselves kindly. Whether we believe that we are at fault, or others are at fault, the undeniable fact is we are hurting. So let's be kind and compassionate and hold ourselves gently, then make room for our feelings and get present.

We will often need to drop anchor repeatedly. Our mind will carry us off to those old events and we will have to bring ourselves back and get present: to engage and re-engage in the here and now. Then once present, we can act in line with our values and infuse our ongoing action with a sense of purpose. We can then take a stand in the face of this reality gap.

For example, if we genuinely did do something 'wrong' or 'bad' or 'careless' — and it's not just the mind being overly critical — then we could now take a stand to make amends. Michael, an alcoholic and Vietnam veteran, told me that in his case this was impossible: he had killed several people in the war and there was no way to make amends for that. Well, it's hard to argue with that, so I didn't even try. Instead I said, 'Beating yourself up and drinking yourself into the grave isn't going to alter the past. And yes, of course you can't make amends to the dead; you can't do *anything* for the dead. But you *can* do something in the present that can contribute in meaningful ways to the *living*. If you waste your life away, then nothing good has come from those horrors of the past. But if you use your life to contribute to others, to make a difference in the world, then something good *has* come out of those horrors.'

For Michael, this was a revelation. It took him a lot of practice, but eventually he was able to unhook himself from those self-blaming stories and treat himself kindly. And over the space of nine months, he joined an AA group, quit drinking, and started volunteering for two charitable organisations: one for the homeless and the other for refugees. Now this wasn't easy for him. It took a huge amount of hard work, and he had to make room for enormous amounts of pain. But it paid off handsomely. Although he couldn't change the past, he found he could make a useful difference in the present — and as he did so, his life became far more fulfilling.

While most of us get entangled in self-blame at times, our stories are probably not as dramatic as Michael's; after all, most of us have never killed someone! However, that doesn't make our stories any less of a burden. The key thing is to practise being kind to yourself (even if your mind says you don't deserve it). It's often useful to say some kind words to yourself, such as: 'I'm a fallible human being. Like every other person on the planet, I make mistakes, I screw things up, and I get things wrong. This is part of being human.' Then place a compassionate hand upon your body, breathe into the pain, and acknowledge it hurts. And remind yourself that self-punishment achieves nothing useful; vitality lies only in taking a stand. If there is something you can do to make amends, or repair the damage, or turn the situation around, then it makes sense to go ahead and do it. If there's nothing you *can* do along those lines (or if you're not yet *willing* to do it), then you can invest your energy in building the relationships you have: connecting, caring and contributing. To do this is an act of self-forgiveness.

But what if someone else did the 'bad stuff'? Well, we could respond in many different ways, depending on the specifics of the situation and the outcomes we are looking for. We might choose to take decisive action to ensure, as best we can, that something like this doesn't happen again: to take that person to court, or lodge a complaint against them, or cut off all contact with them. Or we might choose to learn new skills that equip us better for dealing with such people in the future; this could include anything from self-defence classes, to assertiveness and communication skills, to attending a course on 'dealing with difficult people'. Or we might choose simply to 'put it behind us' and focus on rebuilding our life, here and now.

Forgiveness, then, consists of these three steps: hold yourself kindly, drop the anchor, and take a stand. And the beautiful thing about it is . . . it's never too late.

Chapter 19

IT'S NEVER TOO LATE

I never would have believed it possible — not in a million years. My dad was a fairly typical guy for his generation. He looked after his kids in the traditional ways: he worked hard to pay the bills and ensured that his six children all had food and clothes, a roof over their head and a good education. He was very kind and loving in his own way. And like most men of his generation (and many men of my own), he was terrified of intimacy. And by intimacy, I don't mean having sex; I mean emotional and psychological intimacy.

To be emotionally and psychologically intimate with another human requires two things:

- You need to open up and be real; to 'let the other person in'; to share your true thoughts and feelings instead of hiding them away.
- You need to create a space for the other person to do likewise; to be warm, open and accepting enough that they too can be real and open with you.

My dad never wanted to talk about anything deeply personal. He liked to make intellectual small talk: to exchange facts, figures and ideas; to discuss movies and books and science. This was all well and good — we had plenty of enjoyable conversations — but it meant that I never got to know him very well. I never got to know about the feelings he struggled with, his hopes and dreams, his setbacks and failures, his most important life experiences and what he learned from them. I never got to know what made him frightened or angry or insecure or sad or guilty. I knew virtually nothing of his interior world.

At the age of seventy-eight he developed lung cancer, but he didn't tell me. So, knowing nothing of his diagnosis, I went on a six-week trip overseas. Before I left, my dad had a full head of thick white hair, but when I got back, he was totally bald. He didn't tell me that all his hair had fallen out due to the chemotherapy he'd been having. Instead, he told me he'd shaved off his hair because it was fashionable and he thought it made him look younger. And I believed him.

Of course, as he got sicker and frailer, the true story emerged. But even then, he didn't want to talk about his cancer, or the treatment, or his fears. And every time I tried to talk about it, he changed the subject or went quiet.

Not knowing how long he would live, I tried to tell him what he meant to me as a father: how much I loved him, the role he had played in my life, the ways he had inspired me, the most useful things he had taught me and the fondest memories I had of him. But he was so uncomfortable with such conversations, especially as my eyes would usually brim with tears, that he would end them almost as soon as they started.

Miraculously, he recovered from the cancer. I hoped this brush with death would help him to open up a little, but I was disappointed. He remained as closed off as he'd always been, if not more so.

Three years later, at the age of eighty-one, he had a heart attack. He had major blockages in several coronary arteries and he required open-heart surgery. The operation carried a significant risk of mortality. Talking to him shortly before the operation, I tried once again to share with him what he meant to me as a father. As usual, tears welled up in my eyes — tears of both love and sadness — and he instantly closed off. He turned away and said, in a stern voice, 'Hush now. And wipe away those tears.'

Dad survived the operation, but it knocked him around. He had one complication after another and he spent most of the next year in hospital. Towards the end of that year, he became increasingly weak and more and more demoralised. And yet, he still would not allow me to talk to him on an intimate level. Eventually, he decided he had had enough of life and chose to stop all his medication. Being a doctor himself, he knew exactly what this meant: effectively he was killing himself. Once medication ceased, he knew full well he would have only a few days to live. And even knowing this, he still refused to let me tell him how much I loved him and what he meant to me.

In the last hours of his life, Dad started hallucinating. But in between the hallucinations, he had lucid periods, where for several minutes at a time he would be fully conscious, mentally alert and in touch with reality. During one of these periods, I tried one last time to tell him what he meant to me and how much I loved him. I was a blubbering mess: tears streaming down my face and snot bubbling out of my nose. And to my utter amazement, Dad turned and looked deep into my eyes. His face lit up with a radiant smile, full of kindness and compassion, and he took my hands in his and he listened intently to everything I had to say, never once turning away or interrupting. After I had finished sobbing and blowing my nose and telling him everything I'd been wanting to tell him for years, he said, in a voice full of tenderness and love, 'Thank you.' And then he added, 'I love you, too.'

* * *

I tell this story to make two key points: both of them vital to cover before we end this section. The first is that small changes can have a profound impact. My dad did not transform his personality; all he did was make one small change: he made the effort to stay present and open. And even though the whole episode was over within a few minutes, that one small change gave rise to a beautiful and loving experience that I'll remember fondly until the day I die.

Our society bombards us with the notion that if we wish to find lasting fulfilment, we have to dramatically overhaul our life, or radically transform our personality, or fundamentally alter the way we think (or even do all three!). But the problem is, when we buy into these notions, it doesn't usually help us; commonly, all that happens is we end up placing enormous pressure on ourselves. We push ourselves harder and harder to be different and 'better' than what we are — and we beat ourselves up for not meeting our own expectations. Sadly, rather than raising us up, this just brings us down.

So why not lighten the load? Why not take the pressure off ourselves? Rome wasn't built in a day, and neither was a rich and meaningful life. Why not relax a little? Take baby steps. Go slow. And remember the moral of Aesop's much-loved tale of *The Crow and the Pitcher*: 'Little by little does the trick.'

Trying to make huge changes in a short space of time is almost always a recipe for failure. Occasionally we might manage it, but far more commonly we don't. However, small changes, over time, can make an enormous difference. To quote Archbishop Desmond Tutu: *Do your little bit of good where you are; it's those little bits of good put together that overwhelm the world.*

The second important point of this story is that it's never too late to start making these little changes. Of course, your mind may not agree with that. The human mind is a bit like a 'reason-giving machine': it is brilliant at coming up with all sorts of reasons for why we can't change, shouldn't change, or shouldn't have to change, and one of its favourites is this: 'It's too late! I can't change now. That's the way I am. That's the way I've always been.' But we don't have to buy into such thoughts. Instead of seeing ourselves as 'carved in stone', we can acknowledge that we have a never-ending capacity to learn and grow and act and think differently. All we need to do is tune in to our hearts and ask ourselves: 'What one tiny change could I make? What one tiny change in what I say or what I do or how I think, would take me closer to being the person I want to be?'

I wish my dad had made his change a bit earlier, instead of waiting until he was on his deathbed. But I am so grateful for his precious parting gift: he opened up, stayed present, and allowed me to share my true feelings with him. And he did this *willingly*. It is such a beautiful memory: both heart-warming and heart-rending at the same time. And it's a powerful reminder that as long as we're still breathing, it's never too late to change.

PART 5

FIND THE TREASURE

Chapter 20

IT'S A PRIVILEGE

I once heard a comedian say this as a put-down to a noisy heckler: 'One hundred million sperm — and you had to be the one that got through!' When you think about it in these terms, that it only takes one in a hundred million sperm to fertilise an egg, you realise you are pretty lucky to be alive. When you think about it even more broadly, and consider the chain of events that had to take place in order for you to be here — how your mother had to meet your father, and how their mothers and fathers had to meet each other, and so on, backwards to the dawn of life — it seems almost miraculous that you exist at all. In other words, you are privileged to be alive.

A 'privilege' means an advantage granted to a particular person or group. And an advantage is a condition or circumstance that puts us in a favourable position, or provides us with a valuable opportunity. You are one of a particular group that scientists refer to as *Homo sapiens*, and the fact that you are alive when so many members of your species are dead, puts you in a favourable position. It gives you a valuable opportunity to connect, care and contribute; to love and learn and grow. To treat life as a privilege means to seize that opportunity; to appreciate it, embrace it and savour it.

This is, of course, easy to say, but how do we actually do it?

Well, if you've been applying the principles in this book, you're already well on the way. For just as wood and fire combine to give heat, purpose and presence combine to create a sense of privilege.

Let's come back to the idea that life is like a stage show, and on that stage are all your thoughts and feelings, and everything that you can see, hear, touch, taste and smell. The 'reality gap' is only one part of that stage show. However, when the whole stage goes black — except for one big spotlight on the reality gap — then it seems as if there is nothing to life but our pain. (This is what happens when we fuse with the 'not good enough' story.)

So what if we bring up the lights on the rest of the show? What if we illuminate every aspect? What if we notice *both* the reality gap *and* all the life around that gap? (For no matter how large the gap, our life is larger.) What if, from that space of expansive awareness, we notice the ways in which life is *not* lacking; we notice the aspects that *do* meet our needs and desires? And what if we should discover something very precious? What if we should find some hidden treasure — something that gives us a sense of fulfilment even in the midst of our great pain?

Of course, your mind may say, 'While I have this problem/loss to deal with, nothing else matters' or 'Without X, Y, or Z my life is empty/meaningless' or 'I don't care about anything else'. But if you get hooked by these thoughts, you will get lost in the smog: you will stumble around, scarcely able to breathe. If you want some relief from this smog, you'll need to get present: unhook from those thoughts, cultivate an expansive awareness and notice the whole of your life, not just the 'bad' bits.

What might happen to your life if you were to notice all those things that most of us take for granted? And more than just notice them: *appreciate* them, *savour* them and *treasure* them? Remember B.F. Skinner, treasuring his last mouthful of water? What if you were in this moment to treasure your breathing, or your eyesight, or your hearing, or the use of your arms and legs? What if you were to treasure your next encounter with friends, family or neighbours? Have you ever been for a walk and celebrated the beauty around you? Have you ever breathed in the air and rejoiced in its freshness? Have you ever relished the warmth of an open fire or a comfortable bed? Have you ever savoured a home-cooked meal, delighted in freshly baked bread, or 'loved every minute' of a long hot shower? Have you ever found joy in a hug, or a kiss, or a book, or a movie, or a sunset, or a flower, or a child, or a pet?

At this point, your mind might be saying, 'Yeah, Russ, that's all very well, but what about those people who are stuck in truly horrific circumstances? Surely this isn't relevant to them?' My answer is: first things first. When reality slaps us in the face, first we need to drop anchor and hold ourselves kindly. Next we need to take a stand: if we can't or won't leave, then we change what can be changed, accept what can't be changed, and live by our values. If we've done all that and the situation remains horrific then, yes, it'll likely be very hard to find anything to appreciate, savour or treasure. But it won't be impossible.

For example, in his autobiography *Long Walk To Freedom*, Nelson Mandela describes how during his many years in prison on Robben Island, he was able to savour his early morning marches to the quarry; to appreciate the fresh sea breeze and the beautiful wildlife. Or take the case of Primo Levi, an Italian Jew who was sent to Auschwitz concentration camp for the last year of the Second World War. In his moving book about that experience, *If This is a Man*, Levi describes how he endured backbreaking labour, day in day out, in the freezing Polish winter, wearing only the thinnest of clothes. But when the first days of spring appeared, he was able to truly savour the warmth of the sun. Finally, consider Victor Frankl, another Jewish prisoner in Auschwitz. In his book, *Man's Search For Meaning*, he reveals how even in the midst of all that horror, he was still able to treasure the sweet memories of his wife.

Notice I'm *not* suggesting we try to distract ourselves or pretend the reality gap isn't there. I'm *not* saying we should look at all the other parts of the stage show and ignore the bits we don't like. I'm *not* proposing that we try to think positively and tell ourselves that this is all for the best. (You can try these approaches if you like, but they don't usually work very well — at least, not in the long term.) What I *am* suggesting is simply this: let's bring up the lights on the *whole* stage show. Let's see the gap clearly *and* what's around it *and* also appreciate the privilege of seeing the show. And *then* let's find something in the show that we can treasure.

Of course, like many of the things in this book, this is much easier said than done. Why? Because the default setting of the human mind is to focus on what we *don't* have; on what's *not good enough*; on what needs to be fixed, solved or changed, before we can appreciate life. And although we were sometimes told as children to 'smell the roses' and 'count our blessings', we grew up in a culture that far preferred to focus on the negative, painful and problematic. (If you're in any doubt about that, just open any newspaper and notice what percentage of stories are predominantly negative, painful and problematic.)

This means that when someone suggests we appreciate what we have, our minds may very well be cynical. So if your mind is now protesting, please treat it as if it's a loud voice in the far corner of a café: let it have its say, but don't get caught up in it, or sucked into any kind of argument. And instead let's consider: how *can* we appreciate what we have?

Finding Appreciation

It's actually quite simple to develop appreciation for the things we have. All we need to do is pay attention. But we don't just do this in any old way we want. We pay attention in a particular way: with openness and curiosity. Let's try it now. As you read this sentence, notice how your eyes are scanning the page; notice how they move from word to word without any conscious effort on your part; how they go at just the right speed for you to take in the information.

Now imagine how difficult life would be if you lost your eyesight. How much would you miss out on? Imagine if you could no longer read books, or watch movies, or discern the facial expressions of your loved ones, or check out your reflection in a mirror, or watch a sunset, or drive a car.

When you reach the end of this paragraph, stop reading for a few seconds, look around and notice — and I mean *really notice* — five things you can see. Linger on each item for several seconds, noticing its shape, colour and texture, as if you are a curious child who has never seen anything like it. Notice any patterns or markings on the surface of these objects. Notice how the light reflects off them, or the shadows they cast. Notice their contours, outlines and whether they are moving or still. Be open to the experience to discover something new, even if your mind insists it will be boring.

Then once you have finished, take a moment to consider just how much your eyes add to your life; consider what the gift of vision affords you. What would life be like if you were blind? How much would you miss out on?

* * *

This brief exercise links together all the three P's: presence, purpose and privilege. As we pay attention, with openness and curiosity, we get present. Then we infuse this relationship with purpose: we connect with our eyes; we care about them; and we reflect on how they contribute to our lives and, in turn, we contribute our gratitude. And as we truly appreciate what eyesight gives us — as we treasure the very miracle of vision itself — then in that moment, we get a sense of privilege.

Now as you continue reading, notice how your hands so effortlessly hold this book. When you get to the end of this paragraph, pick up the book, turn it upside down, flip it gently into the air and catch it. Spend a good minute or so playing with the book in different ways. Toss it from hand to hand, or flick through all the pages, or raise it up high and let it drop, catching it before it hits the ground. And as you do these things, pay attention to the movements of your hands. Be curious about them: notice how they know exactly what to do; how the fingers and thumbs work so smoothly together. And be open to the experience; be open to learning from it, even if you really don't want to do it.

**

So, how amazing are your hands? How difficult would life be if you didn't have them? When you reach the end of the paragraph, use your hands to do something pleasant to yourself — gently stroke your scalp, massage your temples, rub your eyelids, or massage a shoulder. Do this for a minute or so, slowly and gently, and again, bring that childlike curiosity and openness to the process; notice how your hands move, and the sensations they generate, and the way your body responds.

Once you've done this, consider how much your hands contribute to your life and how much they enable you to do.

**

Now try another exercise, which focuses on the breath. As you continue reading, slow your breathing. Take a few slow deep breaths and let your shoulders drop. And as you appreciate the simple pleasure of breathing, reflect on the role your lungs play in your life. Consider how much you rely on them. Consider how much they contribute to your wellbeing. Millions of people all over the world have heart and lung diseases that make breathing very difficult — and if you've ever had asthma or pneumonia, you know just how difficult and scary that can be. And maybe you've visited someone in a hospital or a nursing home who was suffering from severe heart or lung disease; their lungs filling with fluid, the only way they could breathe was via inhaling oxygen through a gas mask. Imagine if that person were you. Imagine being in that situation and looking back over your life and remembering when your lungs once functioned well and how much easier your life was way back then. How much do we rely on our lungs and on our breath? And how often do we take these things for granted? Can you, just for a moment, notice your lungs in action and notice the breath flowing rhythmically — in and out — and appreciate how privileged you are to have this experience?

* * *

If we take the time throughout the day to slow down and appreciate what we have, we soon develop a greater sense of contentment. We can do this at any time and in any place. We simply take a few seconds to notice, with openness and curiosity, something that we can see, hear, touch, taste or smell: perhaps the smile on the face of a loved one, or motes of dust dancing in a beam of sunlight, or the sensation of breath moving in and out of our lungs, or the sound of a child laughing, or the smell of brewing coffee, or the taste of butter on toast.

Now I'm not suggesting for a moment that this will solve all your problems. Nor am I asking you to pretend that everything in your life is hunky-dory and that you have no needs, wants and desires. The purpose of this practice is simply to increase our fulfilment. 'Finding the treasure' is a radically different psychological state to our default mindset of lack and discontentment and being fixated on trying to close or avoid the reality gap.

So, next time you drink some water, why not slow down a little and savour the first sip? Swill it once or twice around your mouth and notice how it instantly eases the dryness.

And next time you're out walking, why not take a few moments to notice the movement of your legs: their rhythm, strength and coordination, and appreciate the job they are doing of moving you around.

And next time you eat a delicious meal, why not savour the first mouthful and marvel at how your tongue is able to taste the food, and how your teeth are able to chew, and how your throat is able to swallow?

We all have a tendency to take life for granted, or to forget about all the wonder outside the reality gap. But it doesn't have to be that way. We don't have to wait until we're lying on our deathbed to appreciate the simple pleasure of drinking water. We don't have to wait until our legs stop working to appreciate how they carry us around. We don't have to wait until our eyes and ears fail to appreciate the gifts of vision and hearing. We can appreciate all these treasures, here and now.

Chapter 21

TO STAND AND STARE

When I was about twelve years of age, I had an English teacher who was fond of asking the class to memorise poems. At the time, I absolutely hated having to do this, as I considered poetry to be the most boring thing on the planet (after maths, that is). And out of all the poems we had to learn, there is only one that I remember. I didn't think much of it at the time but, somehow, it stuck in my head and over the years I have really come to appreciate it. It was written by the Welsh poet and writer, William Henry Davies (1871–1940), and I invite you to read it carefully and notice the effect it has on you:

Leisure
What is this life if, full of care,
We have no time to stand and stare.
No time to stand beneath the boughs
And stare as long as sheep or cows.
No time to see, when woods we pass,
Where squirrels hide their nuts in grass.
No time to see, in broad daylight,
Streams full of stars, like skies at night.
No time to turn at Beauty's glance,
And watch her feet, how they can dance.

No time to wait till her mouth can
Enrich that smile her eyes began.
A poor life this if, full of care,
We have no time to stand and stare.

In this poem, Davies cuts to the core of the human condition: we get so caught up in our busy, stressful lives, that we miss out on much that is wonderful. Of course, life also holds plenty that is awful and dreadful; let's not pretend otherwise. However, as Steven Hayes, the creator of ACT, often says: 'There is as much life in a moment of pain as in a moment of joy.' And presence helps us make the most of our living; to find fulfilment in each and every moment: both those full of wonder and those full of dread.

Suppose you are in a lovely, cool, air-conditioned hotel room. You look out through the windows and gasp in admiration at a pristine white beach and the clear blue ocean, as far as the eye can see. The waves are sparkling in the sunlight and palm trees are swaying gently in the breeze. It's a truly spectacular view. But . . . you cannot hear the pounding of the waves, you cannot feel the sunlight on your face, you cannot feel the breeze caressing your face, and you cannot breathe and smell the fresh sea air. This is what it's like to be 'half-present'. You take in some of your experience, but you miss out on a lot of it.

Now suppose you leave your room and step out on to the balcony. Instantly, you feel more alive. You can feel the kiss of sunlight on your skin, the wind gently tousling your hair, and the fresh salty air filling your lungs. This is what it's like to be present: to engage fully in life as it is in this moment and soak up the richness of life; to drink it in and savour it. In the earlier sections of this book, we looked at presence mainly as a means to cope with suffering: to drop anchor, to make room for painful emotions, and to facilitate effective action. But hopefully now you can see that it also allows us to experience life as a privilege.

Moments of Presence

Moments of presence are natural. When we first meet someone we admire or find attractive, we are likely to be very present: we give them our full attention and we hang on their every word. And when we say someone has a 'strong presence', or that we find them 'engaging', what we mean is that they readily and naturally attract our attention. But what of those friends, family and colleagues whom we see all the time: how often do we take them for granted or only half-listen to them? We may even complain about how hard it is to stay present when they 'go on about things' and we may label them as 'boring'.

Similarly, when we taste the first mouthful of a delicious meal in a restaurant, or we smell some delightful new fragrance, or we set eyes upon a spectacular rainbow, for a moment or two we are likely to give it our full, conscious attention. But all too soon, our attention wanes. After three or four mouthfuls of that meal, we start to take it for granted. Yes, we still taste it, but we are no longer savouring it: teasing out the tastes and exploring the textures. Instead, we are eating on autopilot, far more interested in the conversation with our dinner companions than in the sensations inside our mouth. And as for that beautiful fragrance: within minutes it fades into the background, until we hardly notice it any more.

Let's create some moments of presence right now. In the exercise that follows, carry out each instruction for five to ten seconds before moving on to the next.

Mindfulness of Sounds

First 'open your ears' and take a few moments to simply notice what you can hear.

Notice any sounds coming from you (e.g. your body moving in your chair, or your breathing).

Now 'stretch out your ears' to notice the sounds nearby.

Gradually expand your hearing range until you can hear the most distant sounds possible. Can you hear the sounds of the weather or the distant traffic?

Sit still in the midst of all this sound and notice the different layers: the vibrations, pulsations and rhythms.

Notice the sounds that stop and the new ones that start.

See if you can notice a continuous sound of some sort, such as an electrical hum, or the whirring of a fan, and listen to it as if it's a piece of wondrous music. Notice the pitch, the volume and the timbre.

Stay with this noise and notice how it's not just 'one sound'. Notice there are layers within layers, rhythms within rhythms, and cycles within cycles.

Now notice the difference between the sounds you can hear and the words and pictures that your mind tries to attach to them.

* * *

How did you go? Were you able to stay fully present with the sounds, or did your mind pull you out of the exercise? Most of us find the latter. Did your mind perhaps distract you with thoughts like: 'This is boring' or 'I can't do it' or 'Why don't I skip this bit, I don't really need to do this' or 'What's for dinner?'. Or did your mind perhaps conjure up images of the sounds you could hear — of people, cars, birds, or the weather, for example? Or perhaps your mind had you analysing the sounds — 'I wonder what's making that noise?' — or had you identifying and labelling them — 'That's a truck'. Or maybe it just pulled you back to your reality gap: got you worrying about your problems or dwelling on how bad you feel, or wondering how this exercise can possibly help you. Whatever your mind did, it's quite okay; just notice that reaction and let it be.

Lisa and the Frogs

'I can't stand it', said Lisa. 'If I have to listen to those bloody frogs for one more night, I swear I'll go crazy!' A week earlier, Lisa had moved into a lovely new house. Unfortunately, her next door neighbour had a large pond in her back garden, which was home to a family of exceedingly loud frogs. As Lisa described it, the frogs made a noise like two blocks of wood banging together, and they made it all night long. She found the noise intensely irritating and it kept her awake for hours. She'd tried three different types of earplugs, all to no avail, and she confessed — very guiltily — that she'd even started to think about poisoning the frogs.

I took her through the exercise mentioned above, Mindfulness of Sounds, and near the end of it I asked her to fix her attention on the somewhat irritating sound of a lawn mower, which was whirring loudly just across the road from my office. I asked her to be fully present with the sound: to let her mind chatter away in the background like a distant radio and to focus her attention on the sound itself; to notice, with great curiosity, all the different elements involved — the rhythms, vibrations, high notes, low notes, changes in pitch and volume — as if she were listening to the voice of a fabulous singer. Afterwards she reported that the noise quickly shifted from being annoying to rather interesting. She also expressed amazement that she had heard the sound of a lawnmower many hundreds of times, but she had never realised there was so much to it. So I asked her to practise this exercise in bed at night, to listen mindfully to the croaking frogs next door. A week later, she told me, with a huge grin on her face, that she had practised the exercise every night and she now enjoyed the sound of the frogs — she found it soothing and relaxing and it actually helped her drift off to sleep!

Now I'd hate to set you up for unrealistic expectations: presence doesn't always lead to such dramatic results, especially when we're new to it, and the skill is relatively undeveloped. Plus let's not forget that staying present for long is hard to do, because our mind has so many clever ways of distracting us. So if we want to get good at this, there is nothing for it but to practise. Therefore, I'd like to suggest two quick and simple exercises you could easily bring into your daily routine.

Presence With People

Each day, pick one person, and notice their face as if you've never seen it before: the colour of their eyes, teeth and hair, the pattern of the wrinkles in their skin and the manner in which they move, walk and talk. Notice their facial expressions, body language and tone of voice. See if you can read their emotions and tune in to what they are feeling. When they talk to you, pay attention as if they are the most fascinating speaker you've ever heard and you've paid a million pounds for the privilege of listening. (Tip: Choose the person you will practise on the night before and then remind yourself of who it is first thing in the morning. This way, you're more likely to remember.) And very importantly: notice what happens as a result of this more mindful interaction.

Presence With Pleasure

Every day, pick a simple pleasurable activity — ideally one that you easily tend to take for granted or do on autopilot — and see if you can extract every last sensation of pleasure out of it. This might include hugging a loved one, stroking your cat, walking your dog, playing with your kids, drinking a cool glass of water or a warm cup of tea, eating your lunch or dinner, listening to your favourite music, having a hot bath or shower, walking in the park — you name it. (Note: Don't try this with activities that require you to get lost in your thoughts, such as reading, Sudoku, chess or crossword puzzles.) As you do this activity, use your five senses to be fully present: notice what you can see, hear, touch, taste and smell and savour every aspect of it.

* * *

Of course, there are an infinite number of practices that can help us develop presence. Why not invent some of your own? Basically, all you need to do is pick something — an object, activity, or an event — and connect with it. Observe it with curiosity. Take in all the details through your five senses. Then, to accentuate the sense of privilege, reflect on how this contributes to your life. And if you can't think of any way it contributes, then appreciate being alive and having five senses. Or perhaps just simply appreciate having a brief moment to stand and stare.

And stay alert for that old 'not good enough' story — it is always lurking in the background. And if it hooks us, it's like a high-speed shuttle to hell. One moment, we're appreciating life here and now, the next we're deep in the bowels of the earth.

I've taken that shuttle to hell on plenty of occasions. I don't like to admit it, but in the first year after my son's diagnosis, I caught that shuttle many times a day. For example, I'd take him to the playground almost daily, but often he wanted to leave as soon as we got there. He didn't like to climb, he didn't like to swing, he didn't like to see-saw, and he was afraid of going down the slide. The other kids would all be running around, climbing, jumping, laughing, and my son would either be hiding in the corner, or lying on the floor, bawling his eyes out.

Every trip was fraught with anxiety and frustration. But my mind would make it a thousand times worse by comparing my son to the other kids and judging him as *not good enough*. It would point out all the ways that my son was defective, deficient or abnormal; and it would highlight all the fun that the other parents seemed to be having but I was missing out on. (Then later my mind would judge me as *not good enough*, for having such thoughts in the first place: 'What sort of lousy father am I, to have these thoughts about my own child?!') Gradually, over the space of a year, with lots of help from his ABA therapists, my son learned to enjoy the playground, but until he reached that point, I took the shuttle to hell on every excursion.

Now as it happens, there is also a shuttle to heaven. As we defuse from unhelpful stories, make room for our difficult feelings, and anchor ourselves firmly in the present, we start to ascend from the depths and come into the light. And when we go one step further and consciously appreciate what we have, we find that our reality is transformed. The reality gap does not disappear, but it is no longer the centre of our attention; instead of focusing solely on what we lack, we acknowledge and enjoy what we have.

For example, when I let go of all my mind's stories about my son — who he could be and should be, and what he's missing or what's not right — and I love him just as he is, defused from all my expectations and judgements, then the sweetness of those moments is truly wonderful. He transforms from a 'problem' into a 'privilege'. I feel fortunate and blessed that I get to share my life with this remarkable human being, from whom I have learned so much about living and loving. Truly, in those moments, I am 'in heaven'.

Of course, this is the same challenge for all parents: can we unhook from all those unhelpful stories and appreciate our children for who they are and be grateful for all they give us? Indeed, this is our challenge in *every* relationship: with ourselves, with others, and with the world around us. And let's acknowledge that this challenge is a *big* one. Why? Because that shuttle to hell is always waiting. And any one of us can make that trip in a flash.

Fortunately, though, there is always a way to return. The moment we realise we're in hell, we have a choice. We can apply the three P's — presence, purpose and privilege — and instantly turn back the other way.

Chapter 22

PAIN INTO POETRY

When one of my clients, Chloe, was diagnosed with breast cancer, she joined a so-called 'support group'. She had hoped to find a compassionate and self-aware community who could realistically acknowledge just how painful and scary and difficult cancer is, while also providing support and genuine encouragement. But what she found instead was, to use her terminology, 'a bunch of positive-thinking fanatics'. These women did not acknowledge Chloe's pain and fear, instead they told her to think positively — to see her cancer as a 'gift'. They said she should consider herself lucky because this illness had given her a chance to 'wake up' and appreciate her life; a chance to learn and grow and love more fully.

Now personally, I'm all for learning and growing and loving more fully, and this whole book is about waking up and appreciating life. But it's a big leap from that to seeing your cancer as a gift, or considering yourself lucky to have it. And replace the word 'cancer' with 'the death of your child' or 'having your house burned down' or 'being raped' or 'imprisonment in a concentration camp' or 'losing your limbs'. How callous would it be to refer to these events as 'gifts' or to tell people they are 'lucky' when this happens? It is the very opposite of a caring and compassionate response.

All of us have plenty of opportunities to learn and grow and wake up and appreciate our lives; we don't need to have something terrible happen to us in order to do this. And if something terrible does happen, by all means let's learn and grow from it, but let's not pretend that it's wonderful or we're lucky to have it. I've learned and grown a lot through having my son, and I've experienced a huge amount of joy and satisfaction amid all the heartache, but I don't think of autism as a 'gift'.

Having said that, from time to time you will meet or hear of someone who tells you that their illness or injury or near-death experience was the 'best thing that ever happened' to them because it transformed their life in such a positive way. I've met a couple of these folks, and I've read about quite a few others, and the genuine ones are truly inspiring; but my feeling is that these people are few and far between, and most of us will never see things the same way. So why not be honest with ourselves? When bad things happen, let's acknowledge how painful it is, and be kind to ourselves. And then, and only then, let's consider how we might learn or grow from the experience.

So, if you *have* acknowledged your pain, and responded to yourself with compassion, and done what you can to improve the situation, then it may *now* be time to consider several questions. Obviously you didn't ask for your reality slap to happen — life served it up without your consent — but given that it *has* happened, it may well be useful to ask yourself:

- How can I learn or grow from this experience?
- What personal qualities could I develop? *Resilience*
- What practical skills might I learn or improve?

When reality slaps us around, it invites us to grow. And while it's not an invitation that we wanted, if we turn it down, our life is sure to get worse. So how about we accept it and make the most of it? Let's use it to develop defusion, connection and expansion: to get in touch with our values and act with purpose. Let's use it as a rehearsal for the four steps: hold yourself kindly, drop the anchor, take a stand, and find the treasure.

Part of the privilege of life is that we *do* have the opportunity to learn and grow, and we can make use of this opportunity any time we wish to, right up until we take our final breath. So let's be curious: how can we deepen our life in response to distress? Can we perhaps develop more patience or courage? Or compassion, persistence, or forgiveness?

Have you ever heard the old saying: 'When the student is ready, the teacher appears'? I used to cringe at this saying. I saw it as 'New Age' claptrap. I thought it meant that as soon as you were ready for the secret of enlightenment, some guru would magically appear out of thin air. But these days I interpret it very differently. I see it as meaning this: if we are willing to learn, we can do so from literally anything life dishes up. No matter how painful or scary it may be, we can always learn something useful from it.

Personally, in the last three years, I have come to see my son as my greatest teacher. (My mind is telling me that that sounds like an awful cliché, but it is true!) And the lessons come thick and fast on a daily basis. Naturally, I feel very sad when I think about all of my son's challenges; about how much he has missed out on, and how hard he has to try, and how difficult life is for him in so many ways. And I also feel plenty of fear about his future. At the time of writing this book, my son is doing well at pre-school. With the help of a part-time private aide, he is making friends, contributing actively to the class, and generally fitting in well. But we all know very well how cruel kids can be. We know how merciless they can be to children who are 'different'. And I fear that as my son gets older, he will be a target of bullying. Yes, it *may* never happen — and I hope it never does — but there's a very high chance it will. And even to think about that sends a shudder down my spine.

So I have lots of fear and lots of sadness, but mixed with those emotions, I have vast amounts of love, joy and gratitude. It's hard to describe the limitless love I have for my son and the incredible joy he gives me, and the enormous gratitude I feel for having him in my life. Now suppose you say to me, 'Russ, I've got this gadget', and you pull out a little silver box. Right on top of the box is a bright red button and you say to me, 'Russ, this device is amazing. All you need to do is press this red button and all your fear and sadness will completely disappear. However, there's just one side effect. When you press that button, you won't *care* about your son anymore. He'll mean nothing to you. You won't care about how he feels, or how the other kids treat him, or whether he has friends, or what he does after he leaves school. You won't even care whether he lives or dies.'

Do you think I would press that button?

And if our roles were reversed, would *you* press it?

This is what life gives us. If we're going to care about anyone or anything at all, then sooner or later we will encounter a reality gap: a gap between what we want and what we've got. And when that happens, painful feelings will arise. *Those things that really matter also hurt.*

So can we embrace those painful feelings and see them as a valuable part of us? Can we appreciate that they tell us something important: that we are alive, we have a heart, and we truly care?

Can we see our pain as a bridge to the hearts of others? That it spans our differences and unites us in the commonality of human suffering. Only when we know what it's like to hurt, can we relate well to others who are hurting too; only then will we understand the true meaning of empathy. So can we appreciate how pain helps us to build rich relationships: to *connect* with the pain of others, to actively *care* about them, and to willingly *contribute* kindness when they are suffering?

Our emotions are as much a part of us as our arms and our legs. So do we really have to avoid, escape or fight them? Or can we learn to treasure them instead? When our arms and legs get cut, broken or infected, naturally they give rise to pain. But we don't get into a fight with our limbs because of it. We don't wish we could go through life without them. We appreciate what they contribute to our life.

So, let's now consider that part of us that cares. What if we could truly treasure this part and truly be grateful for all it affords us in life? Yes, if we didn't care, we'd have no pain, but we'd also have no joy or love or laughter. We'd go through life like zombies; everything would be pointless or meaningless. There would be no disappointment or frustration, but there would also be no contentment or satisfaction. Our capacity to care enables us to live a life of purpose: to build rich relationships, to motivate ourselves, to find life's treasures and enjoy them. So can we be grateful for it, even though it brings us so much pain?

Let's also consider our ability to *feel* emotions. Can we appreciate the brain's amazing ability to take billions of electrochemical signals coming in from all over the body and decode them and interpret them in an instant, to enable us to feel whatever we feel?

Just imagine if this system didn't work. Imagine if we felt nothing ever again. How much would we miss out on? How empty would life be?

From a mental viewpoint of self-compassion, having dropped anchor and taken a purposeful stand, can we look at these painful feelings inside our body and treat them with kindness and respect? Can we give them space, and give them peace, and give them our caring attention? Can we connect with them with curiosity and openness? Can we reflect on how they remind us of what we care about? Can we let go of judging these feelings as 'bad' and instead cultivate wonder that they exist at all?

I've saved this chapter to the end because it's the hardest thing I am suggesting in this book. To tolerate pain is difficult; to accept it is much harder; but to appreciate it is the hardest challenge of all.

And yet, it is possible. The more we reflect on the privilege of human emotion — that we get to care and to feel in so many different ways — the more we can appreciate *all* our emotions. Yes, this privilege does not come without a price. With passion, comes pain. With caring, comes loss. With wonder, comes fear and dread. But look at the upside; consider what your life would be like without it.

And consider this too: what is the key to lasting fulfilment? What is the essence of human vitality? What is the core of all those things we call 'love'? It is to care, connect and contribute — to live with presence and purpose. Surely there is no greater privilege than this? So I encourage you to make the most of this privilege: to live with presence and purpose. And also to be realistic: to acknowledge that you will often forget to do this. The beautiful thing is that whenever you remember, you have a choice. You can hold yourself kindly, drop an anchor, and take a stand. And right there, in that moment, you will find treasure: the fulfilment that is always there, even when life hurts.

DEFUSION TECHNIQUES AND NEUTRALISATION

Defusion means separating from our thoughts, seeing them for what they truly are, and allowing them to be as they are. There are three main types of strategy for defusion: noticing, naming and neutralisation. Noticing and naming are described in detail in Chapter 6. Neutralising your thoughts means putting them into a new context where you can readily recognise that they are nothing more or less than words and pictures, which then effectively neutralises their power over you.

Neutralisation techniques typically involve either accentuating the visual properties of thoughts (i.e. 'seeing' them), highlighting the auditory properties of thoughts (i.e. 'hearing' them), or both. I encourage you to play around with the techniques that follow, and be curious as to what will happen. You can't accurately predict in advance which techniques will work best for you — any given technique might give you no defusion whatsoever, or it might just give you a tiny bit of defusion, or it could give you a massive amount of defusion. (At times, it could even create more fusion; this is uncommon, but it does occasionally happen.)

Keep in mind that the purpose of defusion is *not* to get rid of unwanted thoughts, nor to reduce unpleasant feelings. The purpose of defusion *is* to enable you to engage fully in life, instead of getting lost in or pushed around by your thoughts. When we defuse from unhelpful thoughts, we often find that they quickly 'disappear', or our unpleasant feelings rapidly reduce — but such outcomes are 'lucky bonuses', not the main aim. So by all means enjoy these things when they happen, but don't expect them; if you start using defusion to try to achieve such outcomes, you will soon be disappointed.

I invite you to try out the following techniques and be curious about what happens. If you find one or two that really help you to defuse, play around with them over the next few weeks and see what difference it makes. However, if any of these techniques make you feel like your thoughts are being trivialised or discounted or mocked, then do *not* use them.

First, on a piece of paper, jot down several of the thoughts that most frequently hook you and distress you. For each technique, pick one of these thoughts to work with, go step-by-step through the exercise, and be curious about and open to whatever happens.

Visual Neutralisation Techniques

Thoughts on Paper

Write two or three distressing thoughts on a large piece of paper. (If you don't have access to paper and pens right now, you can try doing this exercise in your imagination.)

Now hold the piece of paper in front of your face and get absorbed in those distressing thoughts for a few seconds.

Next, place the paper down on your lap, look around you, and notice what you can see, hear, touch, taste and smell.

Notice the thoughts are still with you. Notice they haven't changed at all, and you know exactly what they are, but do they somehow have less impact when you rest them on your lap instead of holding them in front of your face?

Now pick up the paper and, underneath those thoughts, draw a stick figure (or, if you have an artistic streak, some sort of cartoon character). Draw a 'thought bubble' around those words, as if they are coming out of the head of your stick figure (just like those thought bubbles you see in comic strips). Now look at your 'cartoon': does this make any difference to the way you relate to those thoughts?

Try this a few times, with different thoughts and stick figures (or cartoons). Put different faces on your stick figures — a smiley face, a sad face, or a face with big teeth or spiky hair. Draw a cat, or a dog, or a flower, with those very same thought bubbles coming out of it. What difference does this make to the impact of those thoughts? Does it help you to see them as words?

Computer Screen

You can do this exercise in your imagination or on a computer. (For most people it's more powerful to do it on a computer.) First write (or imagine) your thought in standard black lower-case text on the computer screen, then play around with the font and the colour. Change it into several different colours, fonts and sizes, and notice what effect each change makes. (Note: Bold red capitals are likely to cause fusion for most people, whereas a lower-case pale-pink font is more likely to create defusion.)

Then change the text back to black and lower-case, and this time play around with the formatting. Space the words out, placing large gaps between them.
Run the words together with no gaps between them so they make one long word.
Run them vertically down the screen.
Then put them back together as one sentence.
How do you relate to those thoughts now? Is it easier to see that they are words? (Remember, we are not interested in whether the thoughts are true or false; we just want to see them for what they are.)

Karaoke Ball

Imagine your thought as words on a karaoke screen. Imagine a 'bouncing ball' jumping from word to word across the screen. Repeat this several times.
If you like, you can even imagine yourself up on stage singing along to the words on the screen.

Changing Scenarios

Imagine your thought in a variety of different settings. Take about five to ten seconds to imagine each scenario, then move on to the next one. See your thought written:

a) in playful colourful letters on the cover of a children's book

b) as stylish graphics on a restaurant menu

c) as icing on top of a birthday cake

d) in chalk on a blackboard

e) as a slogan on the t-shirt of a jogger.

Leaves on a Stream or Clouds in the Sky

Imagine leaves gently floating down a stream, or clouds gently floating through the sky. Take your thoughts, place them on those leaves or clouds, and watch them gently float on by.

Auditory Neutralisation Techniques

Silly Voices

Say your thought to yourself in a silly voice — either silently or out loud. (It is generally more defusing to do it out loud, but obviously you need to pick the time and place; it doesn't go down well in a business meeting!) For example, you might choose the voice of a cartoon character, movie star, sports commentator, or someone with an outrageous foreign accent. Try several different voices, and notice what happens.

Slow and Fast

Say your thought to yourself — either silently or out loud — first in ultra slow motion, then at super-fast speed (so you sound like a chipmunk).

Singing

Sing your thoughts to yourself — either silently or out loud — to the tune of 'Happy Birthday'. Then try it with a couple of different tunes.

Create Your Own Neutralisation Techniques

Now invent your own neutralisation techniques. All you need to do is put your thought in a new context where you can 'see' it or 'hear' it, or both. For example, you might visualise your thought painted on a canvas, or printed on a postcard, or emblazoned on the chest of a comic-book superhero, or carved on the shield of a medieval knight, or trailed on a banner behind an aeroplane, or tattooed on the back of a biker, or written on the side of a zebra among all its stripes. Or you could paint it, draw it, or sculpt it. Or you could imagine it dancing, or jumping, or playing football. Or you could visualise it moving down a TV screen, like the credits of a movie. Alternatively, you might prefer to imagine hearing your thought being recited by a Shakespearean actor, or broadcast from a radio, or emanating from a robot, or being sung by a rock star. You are limited only by your own creativity, so be sure to play around and have some fun.

Appendix 2

MINDFULNESS OF THE BREATH

This exercise is very useful for developing your mindfulness skills. (You can find it recorded on my MP3 *The Reality Slap,* which can be purchased from www.thehappinesstrap.com.) Before commencing, decide how long you are going to spend on this practice — twenty to thirty minutes is ideal, but you can do it for as long as you wish. (It's generally a good idea to use a timer of some sort.)

Find a quiet place, where you are free from any distractions such as pets, children and phone calls, and get yourself into a comfortable position, ideally sitting up in a chair or on a cushion. (Lying down is okay, but it's very easy to fall asleep!) If you are sitting, then straighten your back and let your shoulders drop. Then close your eyes or fix them on a spot.

For the next five or six breaths focus on emptying your lungs; push all the air out of your lungs and completely empty them. Pause for a second, then allow them to fill by themselves, from the bottom up.

After five or six of these breaths, allow your breathing to find its own natural pace and rhythm; there is no need to control it.

Your challenge for the rest of the exercise is to keep your attention on the breath; to observe it as if you are a curious child who has never encountered breathing before. As the air flows in and out of you, notice the different sensations you feel in your body.

Notice what happens in your nostrils.

Notice what happens in your shoulders.

Notice what happens in your chest.

Notice what happens in your abdomen.

With openness and curiosity, track the movement of your breath as it flows through your body; follow the trail of sensations in your nose, shoulders, chest and abdomen.

As you do this, let your mind chatter away like a radio in the background: don't try to silence it, you'll only make it louder. Simply let your mind chatter away and keep your attention on the breath.

From time to time, your mind will hook you with a thought and pull you out of the exercise. This is normal and natural — and it will keep happening. (Indeed, you're doing well if you last even ten seconds before it happens!)

Once you realise you've been hooked, gently acknowledge it. Silently say to yourself, 'Hooked', or gently nod your head and refocus on your breath.

This 'hooking' will happen again and again and again, and each time you unhook yourself and return your attention to the breath, you are building your ability to focus. So if your mind hooks you one thousand times, then one thousand times you return to the breath.

As the exercise continues, the feelings and sensations in your body will change: you may notice pleasant ones, such as relaxation, calmness and peace, or uncomfortable ones, such as backache, frustration or anxiety. The aim is to allow your feelings to be as they are, regardless of whether they are painful or pleasant. Remember, this is not a relaxation technique. You are not trying to relax. It's quite all right if you feel stressed, anxious, bored or impatient. Your aim is simply to allow your feelings to be as they are, without a struggle. So if a difficult feeling is present, silently name it: say to yourself, 'Here's boredom' or 'Here's frustration' or 'Here's anxiety'. Let it be and keep your attention on the breath.

Continue in this way — observing the breath, acknowledging uncomfortable feelings, unhooking yourself from thoughts — until you reach the end of your allotted time. Then have a good stretch, engage with the world around you, and congratulate yourself on taking the time to practise this valuable life skill.

Appendix 3

VALUES CLARIFICATION

This material is reproduced, with permission, from my book *The Confidence Gap: From Fear to Freedom* (Penguin Group Australia, Camberwell, Vic, 2010).

A Quick Look At Your Values

Values are your heart's deepest desires for how you want to behave as a human being. Values are not about what you want to get or achieve; they are about how you want to behave or act on an ongoing basis.

There are literally hundreds of different values, but below you'll find a list of the most common ones. Probably, not all of them will be relevant to you. Keep in mind there are no such things as 'right values' or 'wrong values'. It's a bit like our taste in pizzas. If you prefer ham and pineapple but I prefer salami and olives, that doesn't mean that my taste in pizza is right and yours is wrong. It just means we have different tastes. And similarly, we may have different values. So read through the list below and write a letter next to each value: V = Very important, Q = Quite important, and N = Not so important; and make sure to score at least ten of them as Very important.

1. Acceptance: to be open to and accepting of myself, ✓ ʃ others, life etc.
2. Adventure: to be adventurous and actively seek, create, or explore novel or stimulating experiences. ✓ I
3. Assertiveness: to respectfully stand up for my rights and request what I want. ✓ I
4. Authenticity: to be authentic, genuine, real — to be true to myself. ✓ I
5. Beauty: to appreciate, create, nurture or cultivate beauty in myself, others and the environment. ✓ I
6. Caring: to be caring towards myself, others and the environment. a
7. Challenge: to keep challenging myself to grow, learn and improve. ✓.
8. Compassion: to act with kindness towards those who are suffering. ✓
9. Connection: to engage fully in whatever I am doing and be fully present with others. ✓
10. Contribution: to contribute, help, or make a positive difference to myself and others. ✓
11. Conformity: to be respectful and obedient of rules and obligations. ✓
12. Co-operation: to be co-operative and collaborative with others. ✓
13. Courage: to be courageous or brave; to persist in the face of fear, threat, or difficulty. ✓
14. Creativity: to be creative or innovative. ✓
15. Curiosity: to be curious, open-minded and interested; to explore and discover. Care - cure - ✓
16. Encouragement: to encourage and reward behaviour that I value in myself and others. ✓
17. Equality: to treat others as equal to myself and vice versa. ✓

18. Excitement: to seek, create and engage in activities that are exciting, stimulating or thrilling. ✓

19. Fairness: to be fair to myself and others. ✓

20. Fitness: to maintain or improve my fitness; to look after my physical and mental health and wellbeing. ✓

21. Flexibility: to adjust and adapt readily to changing circumstances. ✓

22. Freedom: to live freely; to choose how I live and behave, or help others do likewise. ✓

23. Friendliness: to be friendly, companionable, or agreeable towards others. ✓

24. Forgiveness: to be forgiving towards myself and others. ✓

25. Fun: to be fun-loving; to seek, create and engage in fun-filled activities. ✓

26. Generosity: to be generous, sharing and giving, to myself and others. ✓

27. Gratitude: to be grateful for and appreciative of the positive aspects of myself, others and life. ✓

28. Honesty: to be honest, truthful and sincere with myself and others. ✓

29. Humour: to see and appreciate the humorous side of life. ✓

30. Humility: to be humble or modest; to let my achievements speak for themselves. ✓

31. Industry: to be industrious, hard-working and dedicated. ✓

32. Independence: to be self-supportive and choose my own way of doing things. ✓ ✓ ✓ ✓

33. Intimacy: to open up, reveal and share myself emotionally or physically in my close personal relationships.

34. Justice: to uphold justice and fairness.

35. Kindness: to be kind, compassionate, considerate, nurturing or caring towards myself and others.

36. Love: to act lovingly or affectionately towards myself and others.

37. Mindfulness: to be conscious of, open to, and curious about my here-and-now experience.

38. Order: to be orderly and organised.

39. Open-mindedness: to think things through, see things from others' points of view, and weigh evidence fairly.

40. Patience: to wait calmly for what I want.

41. Persistence: to continue resolutely, despite problems or difficulties.

42. Pleasure: to create and give pleasure to myself and others.

43. Power: to strongly influence or wield authority over others (e.g. taking charge, leading, organising).

44. Reciprocity: to build relationships in which there is a fair balance of giving and taking.

45. Respect: to be respectful towards myself and others; to be polite, considerate and show positive regard.

46. Responsibility: to be responsible and accountable for my actions.

47. Romance: to be romantic; to display and express love or strong affection.

48. Safety: to secure, protect or ensure the safety of myself and others.

49. Self-awareness: to be aware of my own thoughts, feelings and actions.

50. Self-care: to look after my health and wellbeing, and get my needs met.

51. Self-development: to keep growing, advancing or improving in knowledge, skills, character or life experience.

52. Self-control: to act in accordance with my own ideals.

53. Sensuality: to create, explore and enjoy experiences that stimulate the five senses.
54. Sexuality: to explore or express my sexuality.
55. Spirituality: to connect with things bigger than myself.
56. Skilfulness: to continually practise and improve my skills, and apply myself fully when using them. ✓ ✓ ✓
57. Supportiveness: to be supportive, helpful, encouraging and available to myself and others.
58. Trust: to be trustworthy; to be loyal, faithful, sincere and reliable. ✓ ✓ ✓ ✓
59. Insert your own unlisted value here. *Endurance . Toler*
60. Insert your own unlisted value here. *. Truthful*

* * *

Once you've marked each value as V, Q or N (Very, Quite, or Not so important), go through all the Vs and select the top six that are most important to you. Mark each one with a 6, to show it's in your top six. Finally, write those six values out below, to remind yourself this is what you want to stand for as a human being.

_____

_____

_____

_____

_____

_____

Appendix 4

GOAL SETTING

Effective goal setting is quite a skill and it does require a bit of practice to get the hang of it.

The method that follows is adapted with permission from 'The Weight Escape' workshops and e-course created by Ann Bailey, Joe Ciarrochi and Russ Harris, © 2010. (Their book, *The Weight Escape*, will also be published by Penguin Books (Australia) in June 2012.) You can download a free pdf of this worksheet from the Free Resources page on www.thehappinesstrap.com.

The Five-Step Plan for Goal Setting and Committed Action

Step 1. Identify Your Guiding Values
Identify the value or values that will underpin your course of action.

_____

_____

_____

_____

Step 2. Set a SMART goal

It's not effective to set any old goal that springs to mind. Ideally, you want to set a SMART goal. Here's what the acronym means:

S= specific (Do not set a vague, fuzzy, or poorly defined goal such as, 'I'll be more loving'. Instead, be specific: 'I'll give my partner a good, long hug when I get home from work.' In other words, *specify* what actions you will take.)

M = meaningful (Make sure this goal is aligned with important values.)

A = adaptive (Is this goal likely to improve your life in some way?)

R = realistic (Make sure the goal is realistic for the resources you have available. Resources you may need could include: time, money, physical health, social support, knowledge and skills. If these resources are necessary but unavailable, you will need to change your goal to a more realistic one. The new goal might actually be to find the missing resources: to save the money, or develop the skills, or build the social network, or improve health, etc.)

T = time-framed (Put a specific time frame on the goal: specify the day, date and time — as accurately as possible — that you will take the proposed actions.)

Write your SMART goal here:

_____

_____

_____

_____

_____

_____

_____

_____

Step 3. Identify Benefits

Clarify for yourself, what would be the most positive outcome(s) of achieving your goal? (However, *don't* start fantasising about how wonderful life will be after you achieve your goal; research shows that fantasising about the future actually reduces your chances of following through!) Write the benefits below:

_____

_____

_____

_____

_____

_____

_____

_____

Step 4. Identify Obstacles

Imagine the potential difficulties and obstacles that might stand in the way of you achieving your goals, and how you will deal with them if they arise. Consider:

a) what are the possible *internal* difficulties (difficult thoughts and feelings, such as low motivation, self-doubt, distress, anger, hopelessness, insecurity, anxiety, etc.)?

b) what are the possible *external* difficulties (things aside from thoughts and feelings that might stop you, e.g. lack of money, lack of time, lack of skills, personal conflicts with other people involved)?

If internal difficulties arise in the form of thoughts and feelings, such as:

_____

_____

_____ then I will use the following mindfulness skills to unhook, make room and get present:

_____

_____

_____

_____

_____

If external difficulties arise, such as:

a)_____

_____

b)_____

_____

c)_____

_____

then I will take the following steps to deal with them:

a)_____

_____

b)_____

_____

c)_____

Step 5. Make a Commitment

Research shows that if you make a public commitment to your goal (i.e. if you state your goal to at least one other person), then you are far more likely to follow through on it. If you're not willing to do this, then at the very least make a commitment to yourself. But if you really *do* want the best results, then be sure to make your commitment to somebody else.

I commit to *(write your values-guided SMART goal here)*:

_____

_____

_____

_____

Now say your commitment out loud — ideally to someone else, but if not, to yourself.

Other Helpful Tips For Goal Setting

- Make a step-by-step plan: divide your goal into concrete, measurable and time-based sub-goals.
- Tell other people about your goal and your ongoing progress: making a public declaration increases commitment.
- Reward yourself for making progress in your goal: small rewards help push you on to major success. (A reward

might be as simple as saying to yourself, 'Well done! You made a start!')

- Record your progress: keep a journal, graph or drawing that plots your progress.

Appendix 5

ABA, RFT AND CHILD DEVELOPMENT

In the field of autism and 'special needs' children, therapies derived from Applied Behaviour Analysis (ABA) have major advantages over other treatment methods. ABA's main strengths include:

 a) clearly measurable outcomes
 b) the ability to be closely tailored to the needs of the individual
 c) strong foundations in the basic science of how humans learn from and interact with their world.

As mentioned in Chapter 17, ABA programmes basically treat autism as a skills deficit. The autistic child typically has major deficits in most or all of the following areas: thinking skills, language/communication skills, play skills, social skills and attention skills. The therapists help the child to develop these skills by breaking them down into tiny simple steps, and practising them over and over, with massive amounts of encouragement and reward. The best researched and most widely disseminated ABA programme is the 'Lovaas Program'. About 90 per cent of autistic children make significant improvements with this programme. Better still, 50 per cent of these children improve so much they reach normal intellectual and educational functioning, with an average or above-average IQ, and are indistinguishable from their peers to an outside observer.

Not surprisingly then, ABA is considered best practice by those professionals who are committed to using evidence-based approaches. Indeed, in 2010, the American Academy of Pediatrics proclaimed ABA as the *only* treatment for autism with strong evidence to support its effectiveness. It is very sad that most governments in the world today do not realise the enormous benefits to their country that would come from publicly funding ABA programmes. The one exception I know of is Canada. The Canadian government funds ABA for all autistic children up to age seven; on average, it costs the government half a million dollars per child, but it saves them about four million dollars in long-term health costs. You don't need to be a mathematical genius to see the implications of these figures.

However, ABA is not without its opponents and critics. Sadly, most of these people base their criticisms on what ABA used to be like forty years ago. I personally find this bizarre; imagine criticising the treatment of a modern-day doctor based on what her predecessors did forty years ago! The opponents of ABA seem to be unaware that the programmes have changed enormously over the decades, and they no longer resemble the programmes of yesteryear. In particular, they no longer include any use of 'aversives' (unpleasant stimuli to reduce unwanted behaviour) and the skills training is now often carried out in a naturalistic manner across many different environments (as opposed to keeping the child 'glued' to the table top).

Nonetheless, some criticisms of ABA are fair; the undeniable truth is, despite its effectiveness, ABA has had its drawbacks. Until very recently, practitioners were unable to write programmes based on ABA principles that could effectively target theory of mind, inferential thought, perspective-taking, emotional awareness, compassion and empathy; nor could they generate the extraordinary speed of language learning we see in normal children. All this has now changed with the development of RFT (Relational Frame Theory). RFT is a revolutionary theory of language and cognition, which is too complex to explain quickly and simply in an appendix. However, in the last twenty years, more than 180 articles on RFT have been published in top scientific journals: an impressive body of scientific evidence by any standard.

RFT adds a new level of analysis that now allows ABA practitioners to write programmes that effectively target the issues mentioned above, while also maintaining ABA's scientific rigour, solid evidence base, and measurable evidence of outcomes. As a result of RFT analysis, we can now see deeper into a child's developmental needs and design interventions that are faster, more efficient and have much greater impact. More importantly, RFT and the 'third wave' behavioural interventions (such as ACT) have articulated what the requirements of normal development are: the capacity and skills to be flexible, experientially aware, and empowered to move in valued direction.

Any ABA therapist wishing to learn about RFT and its applications to autism would do well to start with the introductory textbook *Learning RFT: An Introduction to Relational Frame Theory and Its Clinical Application* by Niklas Törneke. Then, once the basics of RFT are understood, you could move on to *Derived Relational Responding Applications for Learners with Autism and Other Developmental Disabilities* by Ruth Anne Rehfeldt and Yvonne Barnes-Holmes.

Psychologist Darin Cairns is arguably the world's leading expert on the use of RFT with autism; he can be contacted at: darincairns@gmail.com.

RESOURCES

Books by Russ Harris

The Happiness Trap (Robinson, 2008)

Many popular notions of happiness are misleading, inaccurate and will actually make you miserable if you believe them. *The Happiness Trap* is a self-help book written for everyone and anyone on how to make life richer, fuller and more meaningful, while avoiding common 'happiness traps'. Based on ACT (Acceptance and Commitment Therapy), it is applicable to everything from work stress and addictions, to anxiety and depression, to the pressures of parenting and the challenges of terminal illness. Widely used by ACT therapists and their clients all around the world, *The Happiness Trap* is currently translated into twenty-two languages. Go to www.thehappinesstrap.com for free resources to use with the book.

ACT with Love: Stop Struggling, Reconcile Differences, and Strengthen your Relationship with Acceptance and Commitment Therapy (New Harbinger Publications, Oakland, CA, 2009)

ACT with Love is a self-help book that aims to inspire and empower readers through applying the principles of ACT to common relationship issues, and shows how to move from conflict, struggle and disconnection to forgiveness, acceptance, intimacy and genuine loving. There are many free resources to use with this book at www.thehappinesstrap.com.

The Confidence Gap: From Fear to Freedom (Robinson, 2011)

Is there a gap between where you are right now and where you want to be? Is a lack of confidence holding you back? We've all been stuck in the 'confidence gap': we want to find a better job, pursue a romantic relationship, enrol on a course, expand our business, or pursue our greatest dreams, but fear gets in the way and we don't take action. Using the principles of ACT, I have helped thousands of people overcome fear and develop genuine confidence — and this book reveals how it is done. *The Confidence Gap* will help you identify your passions, succeed at your challenges and create a life that is truly fulfilling.

ACT Made Simple: An Easy-to-read Primer on Acceptance and Commitment Therapy (New Harbinger Publications, Oakland, CA, 2009)

This is a practical and accessible textbook for psychologists, counsellors and coaches that is equally useful for experienced ACT practitioners and total newcomers to the approach. *ACT Made Simple* offers clear explanations of the core ACT processes and real-world tips and solutions for rapidly and effectively implementing them in your coaching or therapy practice. Reading this book is all the training you need to begin using ACT techniques with your clients for impressive results. There are many free resources to use with the textbook, available from www.thehappinesstrap.com.

CDs and MP3s by Russ Harris

The Reality Slap: Exercises from the Book

Available as a downloadable MP3 file from www.the happinesstrap.com, this volume includes all-new recordings to accompany the written exercises from the book. You'll find a range of powerful exercises to help you develop mindfulness skills, self-compassion, forgiveness and loving kindness. Except for one track (mindful breathing), these exercises are all very different to my first two 'albums': *Mindfulness Skills: Volume 1* and *Mindfulness Skills: Volume 2*.

Mindfulness Skills: Volume 1 and Volume 2

Available as either CDs or downloadable MP3 files, these two volumes cover a wide range of mindfulness exercises for personal use. You can order MP3s via www.thehappiness trap.com. The CDs are only available in Australia and must be ordered through www.actmindfully. com.au.

Online Resources

The Reality Slap is linked to the website www.thehappiness trap.com. On this site, under the Free Resources section, you can download free copies of the exercises and worksheets within these pages. You'll also find some valuable online training in the form of e-courses and webinars.

Newsletter

The Happiness Trap Newsletter is a regular, free e-mail, packed with useful information, tools and tips relating to ACT. You can register for the mailing list under the main menu at any of the websites mentioned above.

ACKNOWLEDGEMENTS

First and foremost, I am deeply indebted and incredibly grateful to my wife, Carmel, for all her love, support, patience and encouragement; for her many useful ideas and suggestions; and for keeping the family living and thriving when I was so bogged down in my work.

Next, a planet-sized amount of thanks to Steven Hayes, the originator of ACT, for not only introducing this amazing model to the world, but also for all his help and encouragement with my books and my career. And that gratitude also extends to the larger ACT community worldwide, which is always very supportive, giving and caring.

Third, a huge amount of gratitude goes to my agent, Sammie Justesen, for all her continuing good work.

Fourth, my thanks to Joe Ciarrochi and Ann Bailey for allowing me to use the goal-setting materials from our 'Weight Escape' programme in Appendix 4.

And last but not least, several truckloads of thanks to the entire team at my Australian publishers, Exisle Publishing — especially Benny Thomas, Gareth St John Thomas, Penny Capp, Anouska Jones and Monica Berton — for all the hard work, care and attention they have invested not just in this book, but also in my earlier works.

ACKNOWLEDGEMENTS

INDEX

RUSS HARRIS

THE
HAPPINESS
TRAP

Based on ACT:
A revolutionary
mindfulness-based
programme for overcoming
stress, anxiety and depression

'This book could save you years of psychological struggle,
yank you out of negative emotional patterns, and help
propel you to a much happier, more productive life.'
Martha Beck, author of *Finding Your Own North Star*

Do you ever feel worried, miserable or unfulfilled – yet put on a happy face and pretend everything's fine? You are not alone. Stress, anxiety, depression and low self-esteem are all around. New research suggests that many of us get caught in a psychological trap, a vicious circle in which the more we strive for happiness, the more it eludes us.

Fortunately, there is a way to escape from the 'Happiness Trap'. Using the six principles of Acceptance and Commitment Therapy (ACT), Russ Harris can help you to:

- reduce stress and worry
- rise above fear, doubt and insecurity
- handle painful thoughts and feelings more effectively
- break self-defeating habits
- improve performance and find fulfilment in your work
- build more satisfying relationships
- create a richer and more meaningful life

978-1-84529-825-8
£9.99

Visit www.constablerobinson.com for more information

Closing the gap with
consistent Industry in
ART creation — and
Act Psychology -
De-fusion -
Presence -

Goal: Master De-fusion
by end of June 2014-